IN THE HEIGHTS

ISBN 978-1-70514-345-2

WARNER CHAPPELL MUSIC

EXCLUSIVELY DISTRIBUTED BY

HAL•LEONARD®

Visit Hal Leonard Online at
www.halleonard.com

Contact us:
Hal Leonard
7777 West Bluemound Road
Milwaukee, WI 53213
Email: info@halleonard.com

In Europe, contact:
Hal Leonard Europe Limited
42 Wigmore Street
Marylebone, London, W1U 2RN
Email: info@halleonardeurope.com

In Australia, contact:
Hal Leonard Australia Pty. Ltd.
4 Lentara Court
Cheltenham, Victoria, 3192 Australia
Email: info@halleonard.com.au

IN THE HEIGHTS

Music and Lyrics by
LIN-MANUEL MIRANDA

Hip-Hop, half-time feel

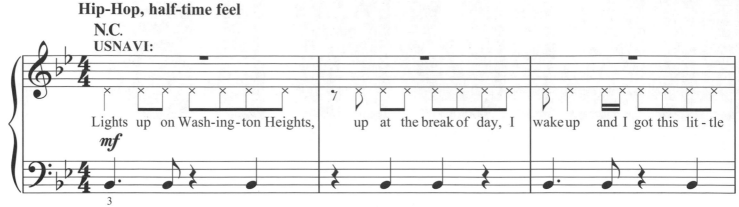

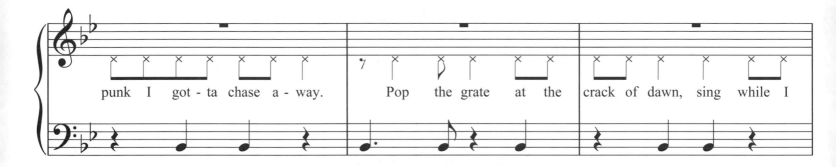

ex - ac - er - bat - ed by the fact that my syn - tax is high - ly com - pli - cat - ed 'cuz I

im - mi - grat - ed from the sin - gle great - est lit - tle place in the Car - ib - be - an: Do - min - i - can Re -

pub - lic! I love it! Je - sus, I'm jeal - ous of it. And be - yond that, ev - er since my

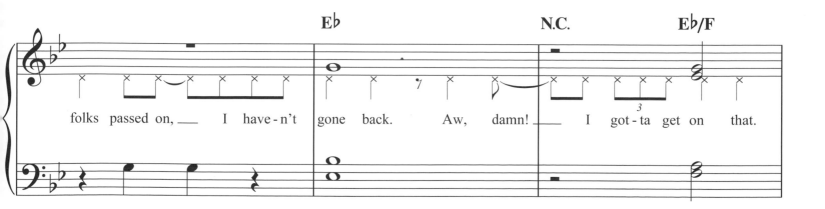

folks passed on, ___ I have - n't gone back. Aw, damn! ___ I got - ta get on that.

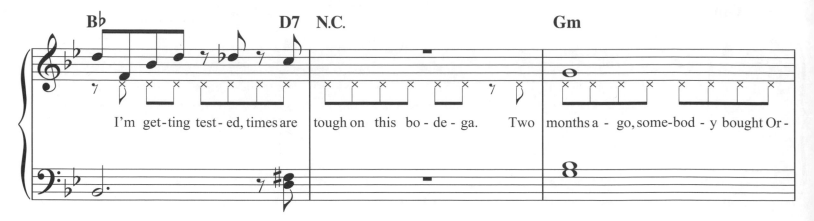

Bb   **D7**   **N.C.**   **Gm**

I'm get-ting test-ed, times are | tough on this bo-de-ga.   Two | months a-go, some-bod-y bought Or-

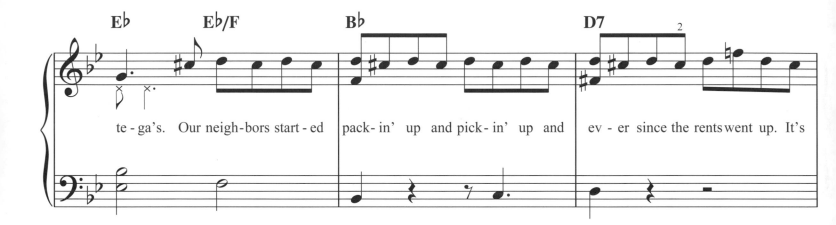

Eb   **Eb/F**   **Bb**   **D7**

te - ga's. Our neigh-bors start-ed | pack-in' up and pick-in' up and | ev - er since the rents went up. It's

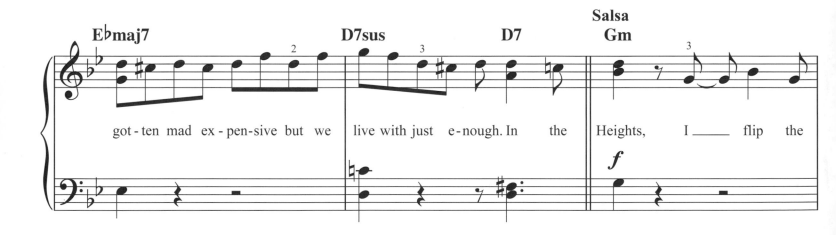

Ebmaj7   **D7sus**   **D7**   **Salsa**   **Gm**

got - ten mad ex - pen-sive but we | live with just e-nough. In   the | Heights,   I ___ flip   the

f

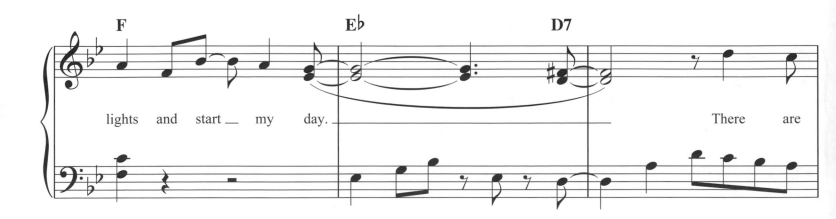

F   **Eb**   **D7**

lights   and start ___ my   day. ___ | | There   are

fights and end - less debts _____ and bills to pay. _____

_____ In the Heights, I _____ can't sur - vive with - out _____ ca - fé, _____

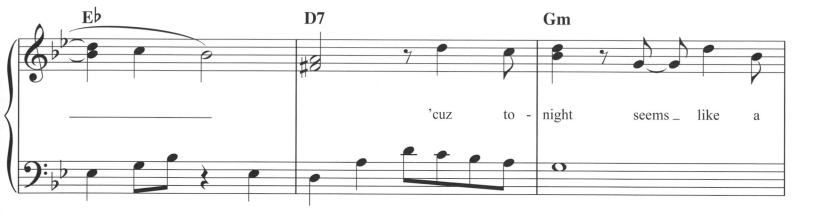

_____ 'cuz to - night seems _ like a

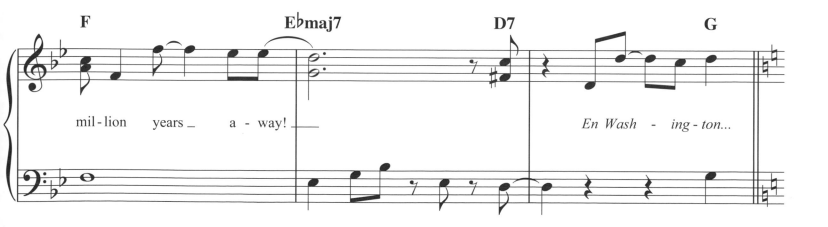

mil - lion years _ a - way! _____ *En Wash - ing - ton...*

Hip-Hop

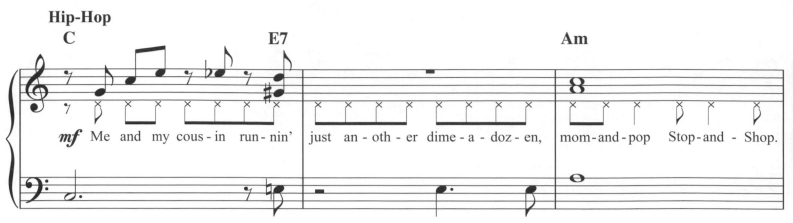

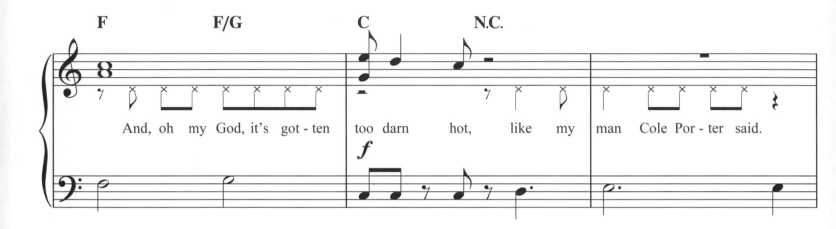

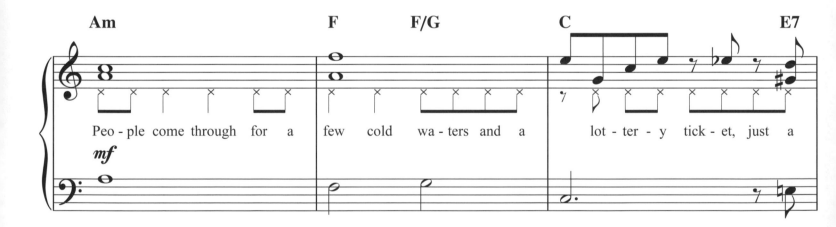

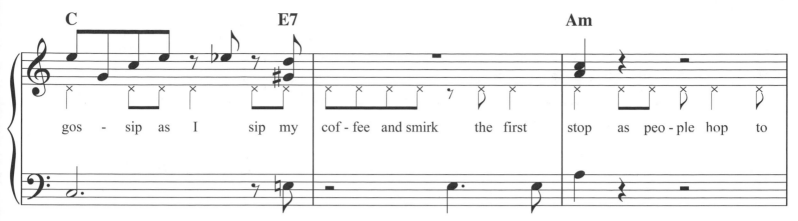

C   **E7**   **Am**

gos - sip as I sip my cof - fee and smirk the first stop as peo - ple hop to

Dance-Hall Reggae

G/A   **C**   **E7**

work, bust it. I'm like, "One dol - lar, two dol - lars, one fif - ty, one six - ty -

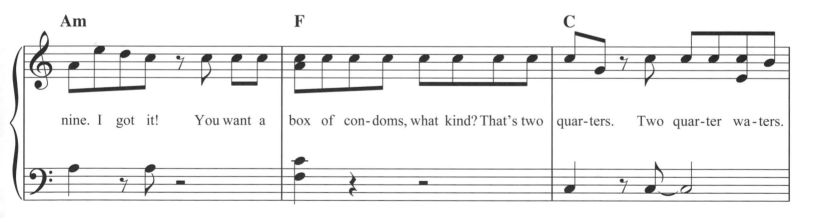

Am   **F**   **C**

nine. I got it! You want a box of con - doms, what kind? That's two quar - ters. Two quar - ter wa - ters.

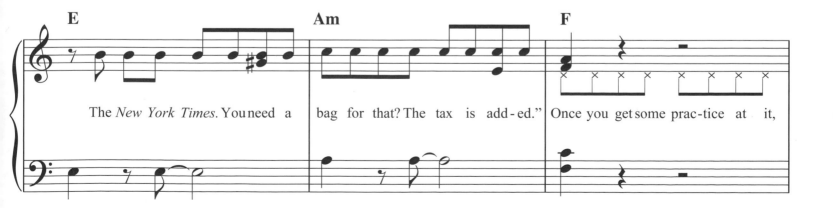

E   **Am**   **F**

The *New York Times.* You need a bag for that? The tax is add - ed." Once you get some prac - tice at it,

8

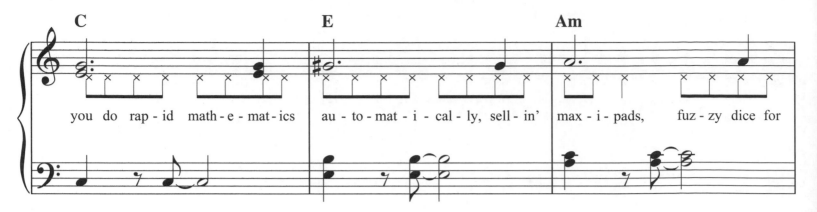

you do rap - id math - e - mat - ics au - to - mat - i - cal - ly, sell - in' max - i - pads, fuz - zy dice for

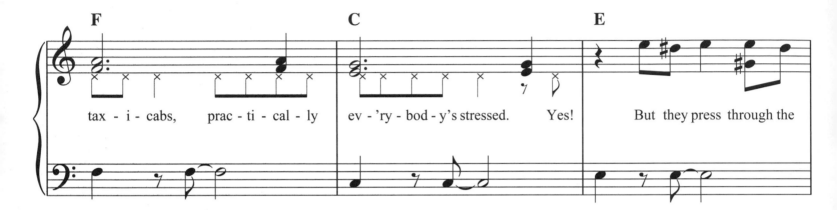

tax - i - cabs, prac - ti - cal - ly ev - 'ry - bod - y's stressed. Yes! But they press through the

mess, bounce checks and won - der what's next. In the Heights, I ____ buy my

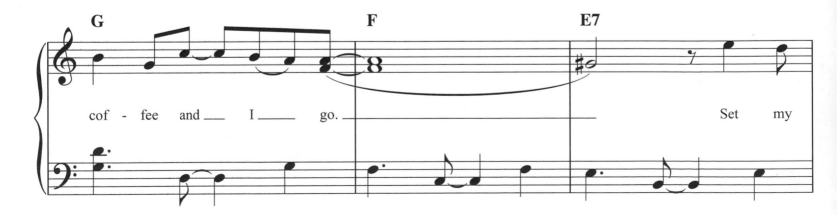

cof - fee and ___ I ___ go. ____ Set my

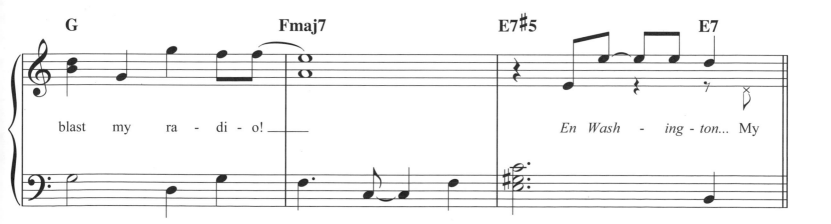

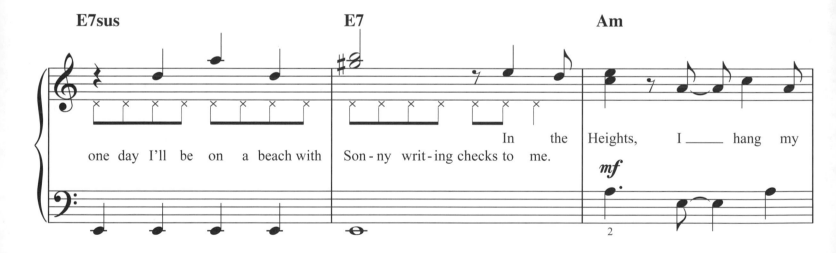

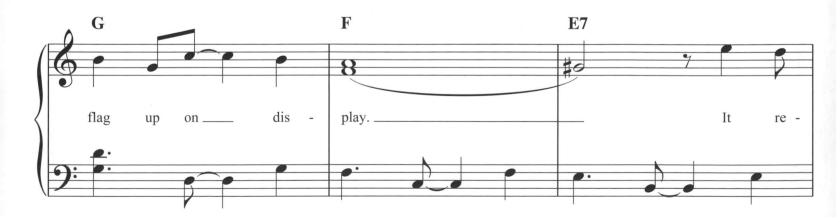

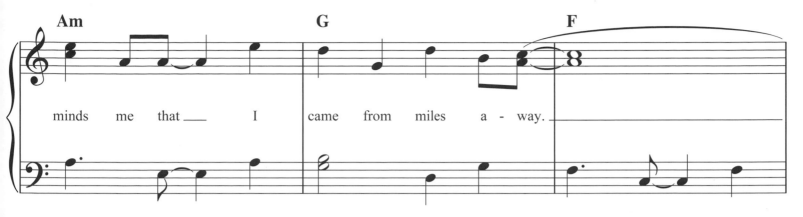

minds me that ___ I came from miles a - way. ___

___ In the Heights, it gets ___ more ex - pen - sive ev - 'ry

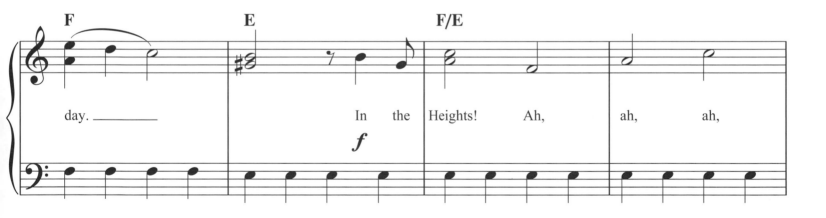

day. ___ In the Heights! Ah, ah, ah,

ah! *En Wash - ing - ton Heights!*

BREATHE

Music and Lyrics by
LIN-MANUEL MIRANDA

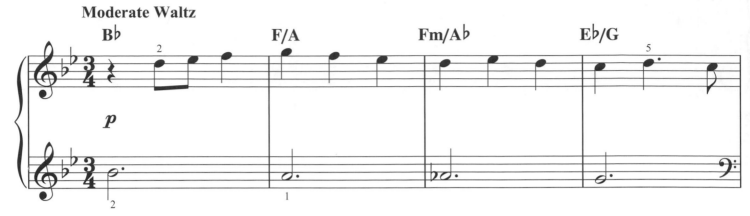

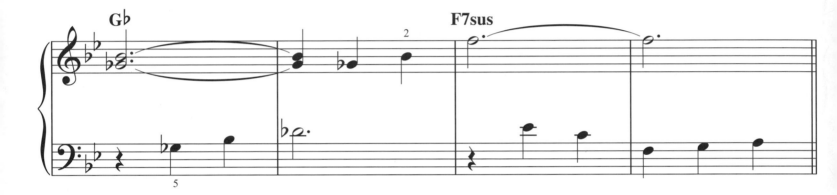

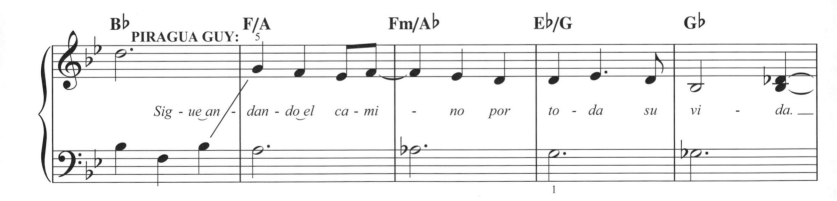

PIRAGUA GUY: Sig - ue an / - dan - do el ca - mi - no por to - da su vi - da. __

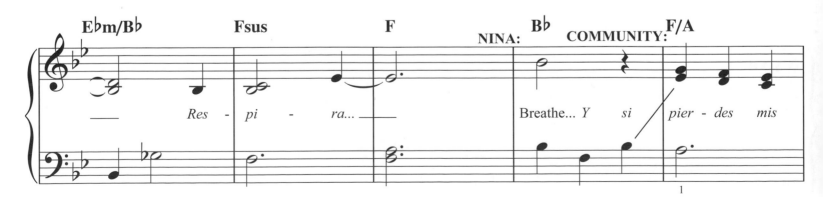

Res - pi - ra... __ NINA: Breathe... Y si / pier - des mis

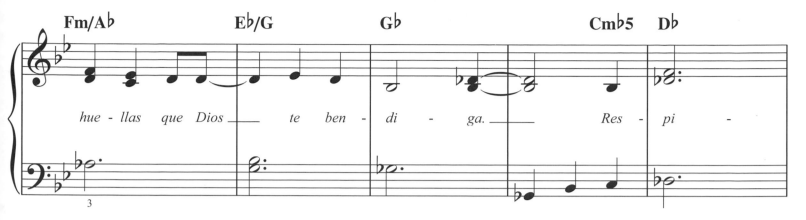

huellas que Dios te bendiga. Res - pi -

ra... **NINA:** This is my street. I smile at the fac -

- es I've known all my life. They re - gard me with pride. And

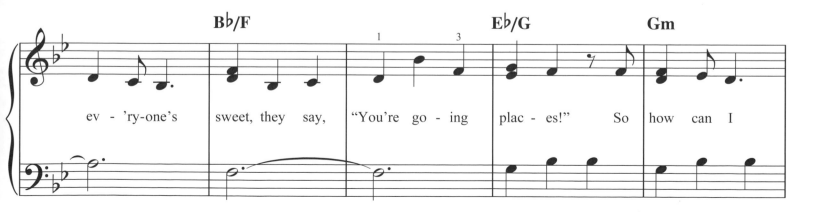

ev - 'ry-one's sweet, they say, "You're go - ing plac - es!" So how can I

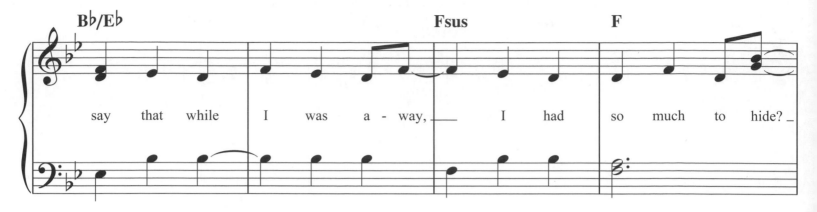

say that while I was a - way, ___ I had so much to hide? _

__ "Hey guys, it's me! The big - gest dis - ap -

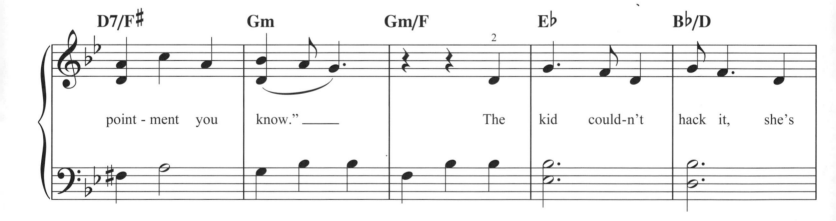

point - ment you know." ___ The kid could-n't hack it, she's

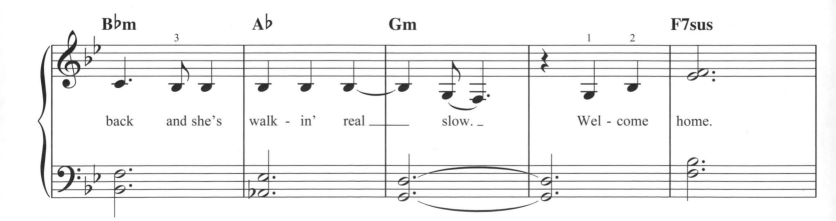

back and she's walk - in' real ___ slow. _ Wel - come home.

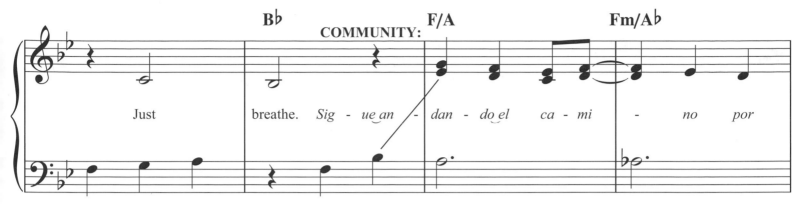

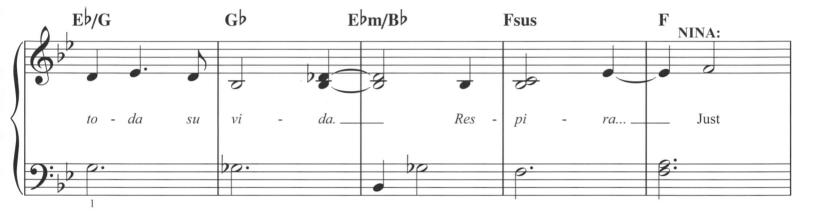

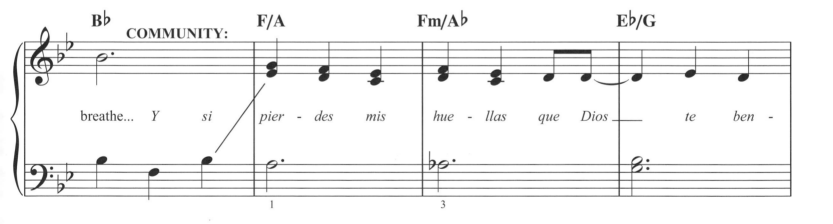

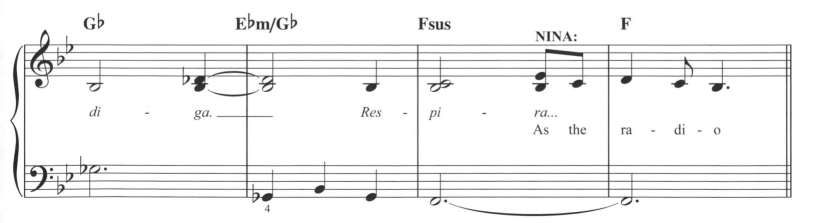

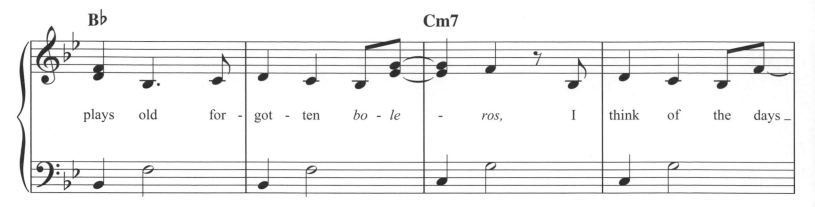

plays old for - got - ten *bo - le - ros,* I think of the days

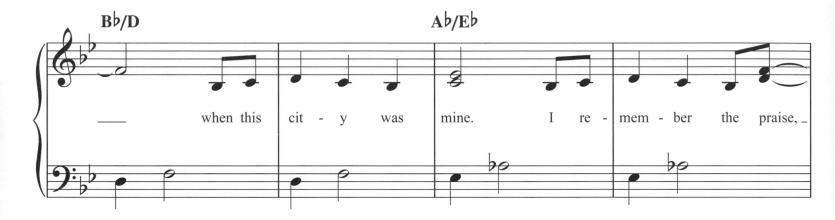

when this cit - y was mine. I re - mem - ber the praise,

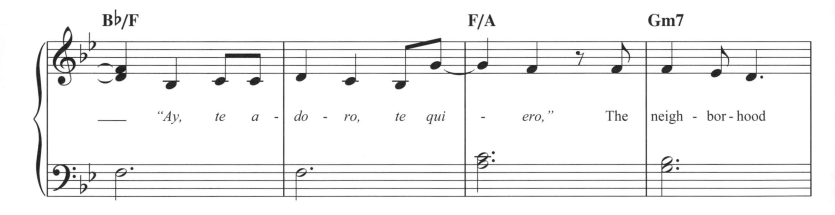

"Ay, te a - do - ro, te qui - ero," The neigh - bor - hood

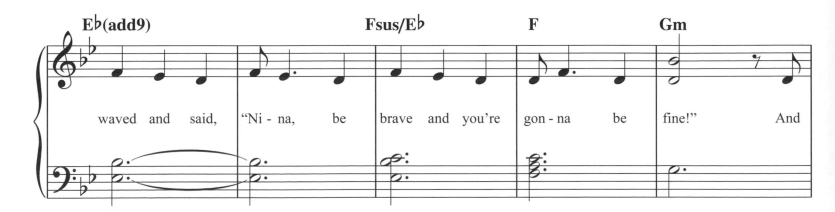

waved and said, "Ni - na, be brave and you're gon - na be fine!" And

may - be it's me, but it all seems like life - times a -

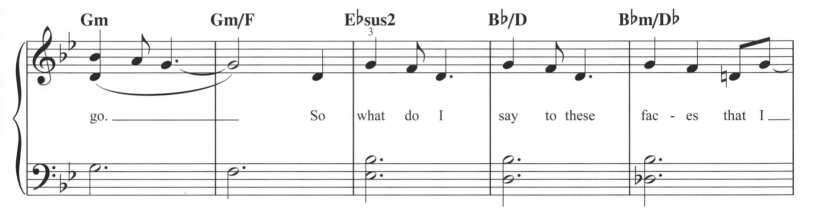

go. So what do I say to these fac - es that I

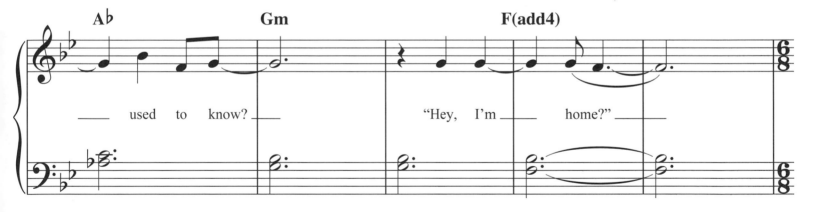

used to know? "Hey, I'm home?"

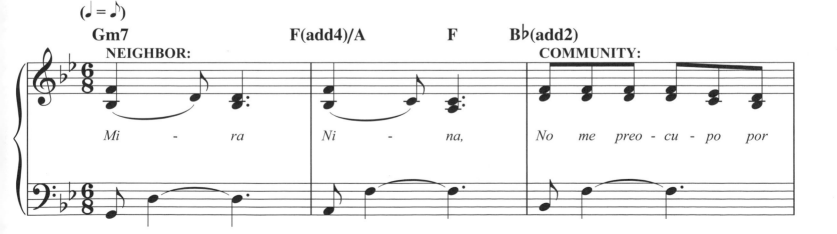

Mi - ra Ni - na, No me preo - cu - po por

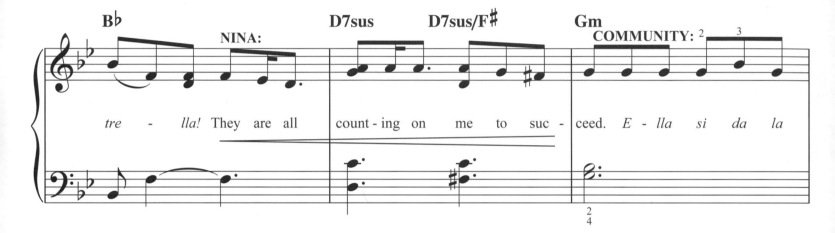

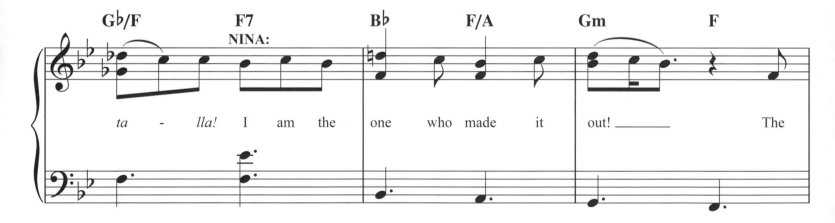

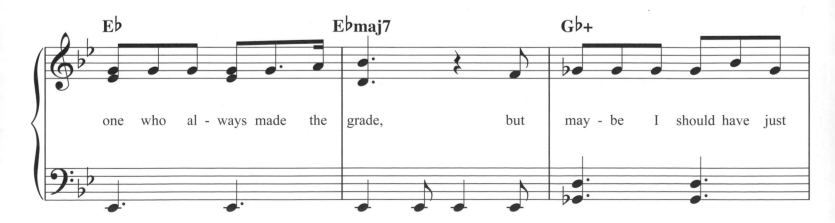

Gm / Fsus

stayed home._ When I was a child_ I stayed wide a-wake, climbed to the

Eb / D / D7/F# / Gm

high-est place on ev-'ry fire es-cape, rest-less to climb._ I got ev-'ry

Eb / Bb / D7 / D7/F#

schol-ar-ship, saved ev-'ry dol-lar, the first to go to col-lege, how do I tell them

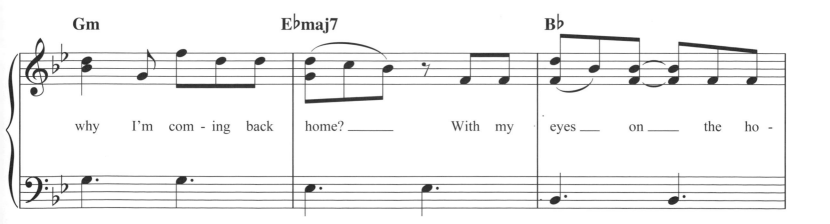

Gm / Ebmaj7 / Bb

why I'm com-ing back home?____ With my eyes__ on__ the ho-

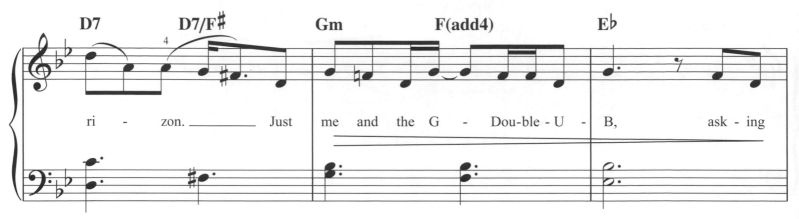

ri - zon. _____ Just me and the G - Dou-ble - U - B, ask - ing

"Gee, Ni - na, what - 'll you be?" _____ Straight - en the

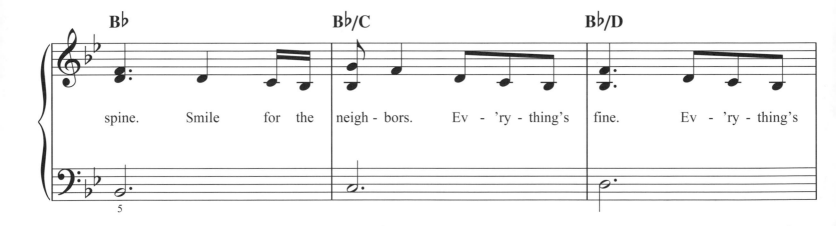

spine. Smile for the neigh - bors. Ev - 'ry - thing's fine. Ev - 'ry - thing's

cool. The stan - dard re - ply: _____ "Lots of tests, lots of pa - pers." Smile, wave good - bye _____

and pray to the sky. Oh, God! __ And what will my par-ents say? __

__ Can I go in there __ and say, __ "I

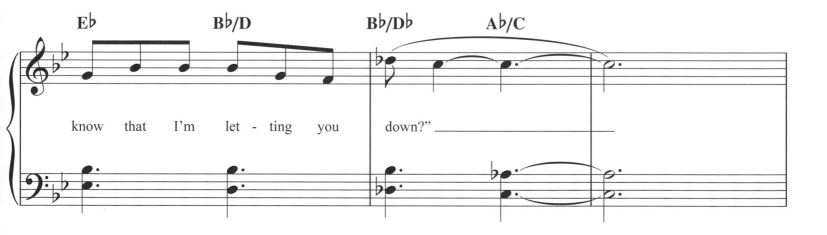

know that I'm let-ting you down?" _____

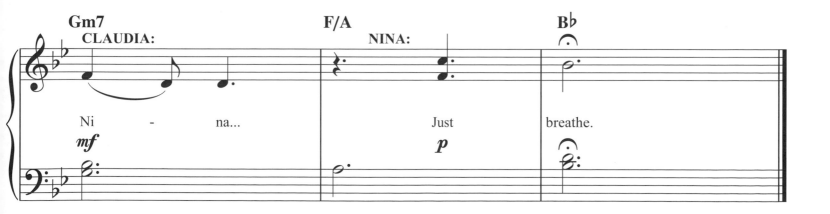

CLAUDIA:
Ni - na...

NINA:
Just breathe.

IT WON'T BE LONG NOW

Music and Lyrics by
LIN-MANUEL MIRANDA

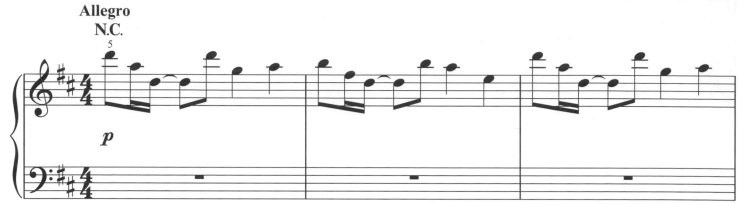

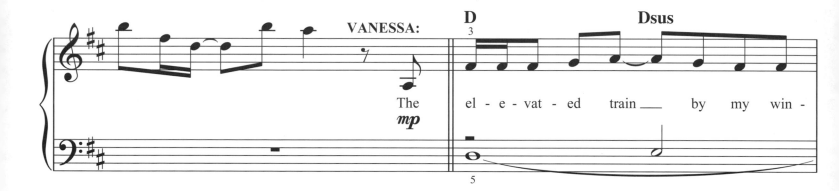

VANESSA: The el-e-vat-ed train by my win-

dow does-n't faze me an-y-more. The

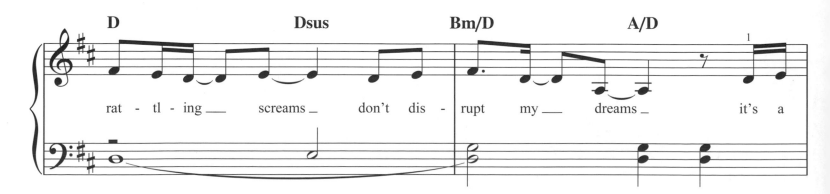

rat-tl-ing screams don't dis-rupt my dreams it's a

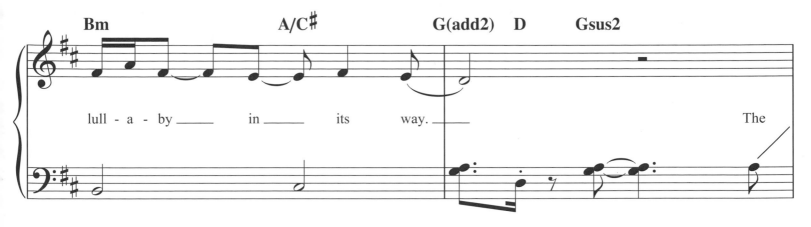

lull - a - by _____ in _____ its _____ way. _____ The

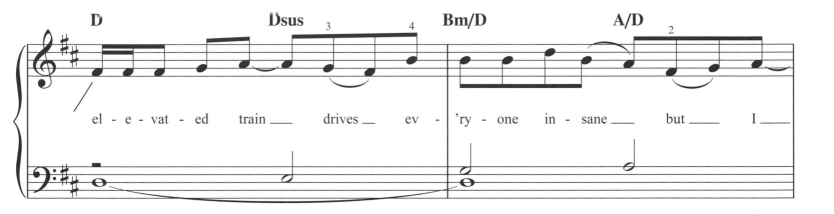

el - e - vat - ed train _____ drives _____ ev - 'ry - one in - sane _____ but _____ I _____

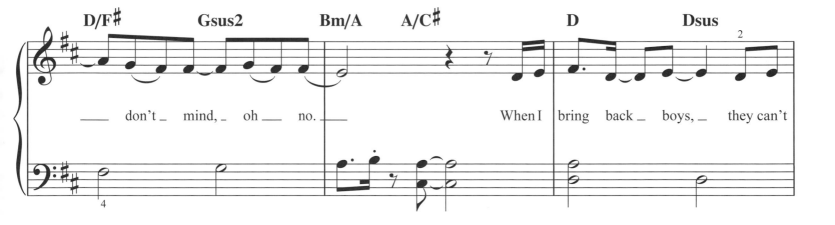

_____ don't _ mind, _ oh _ no. _____ When I bring back _ boys, _ they can't

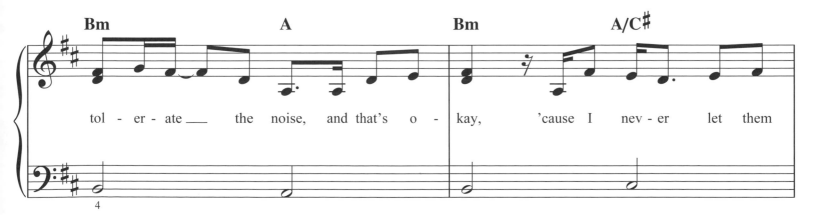

tol - er - ate _____ the noise, and that's o - kay, 'cause I nev - er let them

24

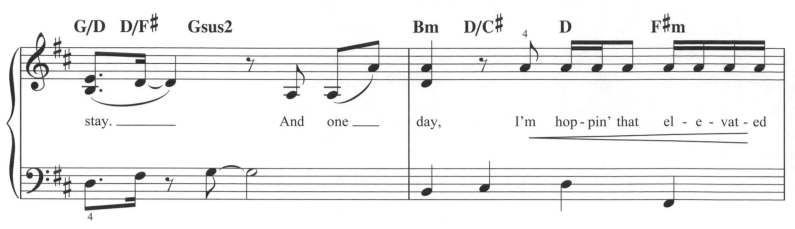

stay. _____ And one ___ day, I'm hop-pin' that el-e-vat-ed

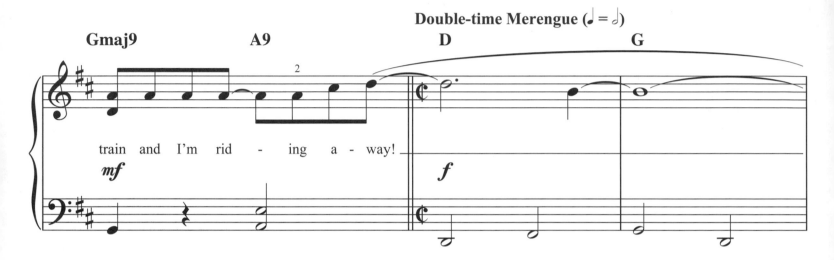

train and I'm rid - ing a - way!

Double-time Merengue (♩ = ♪)

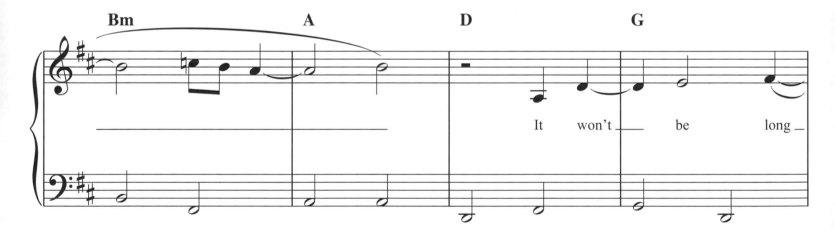

It won't ___ be long ___

now! ___ The

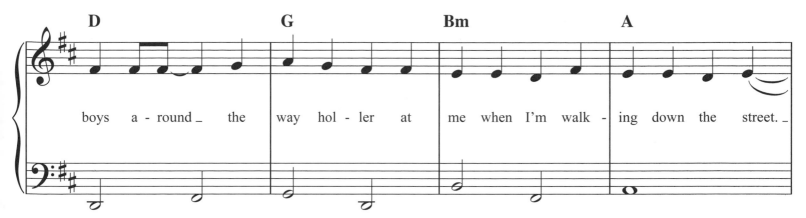

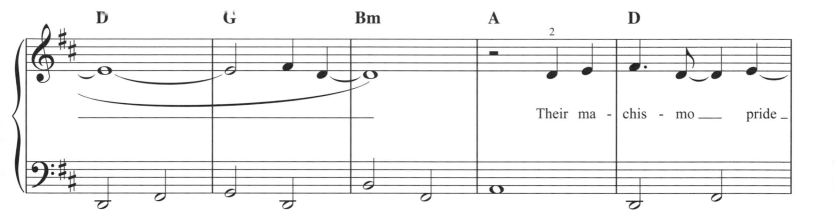

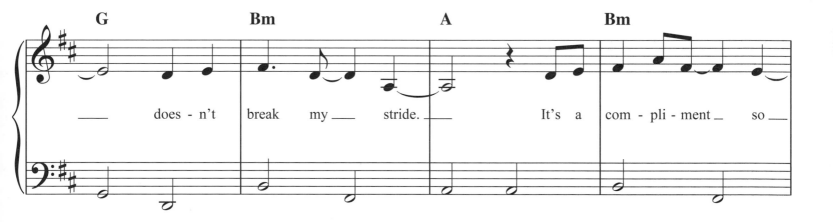

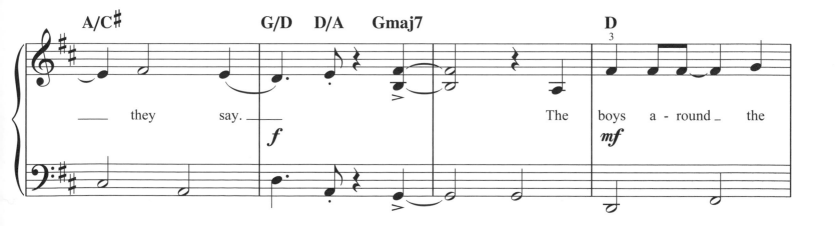

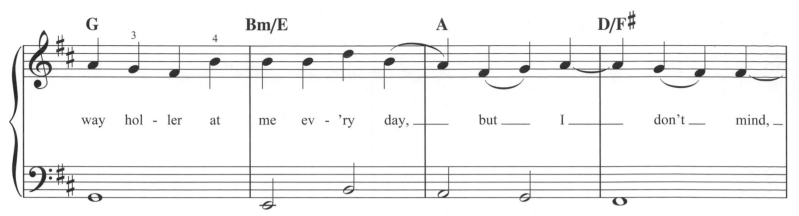

way hol - ler at me ev - 'ry day, ___ but ___ I ___ don't ___ mind,

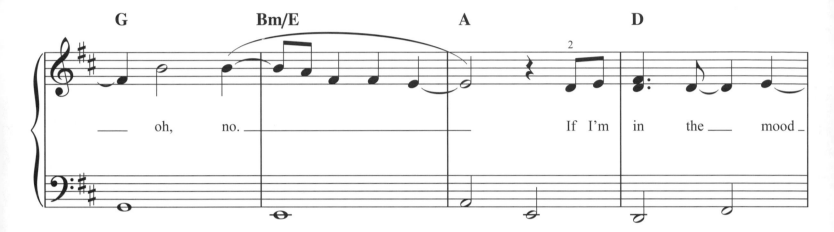

___ oh, no. ___ If I'm in the ___ mood

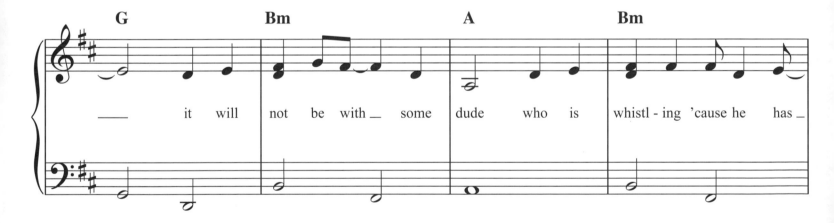

___ it will not be with ___ some dude who is whistl - ing 'cause he has ___

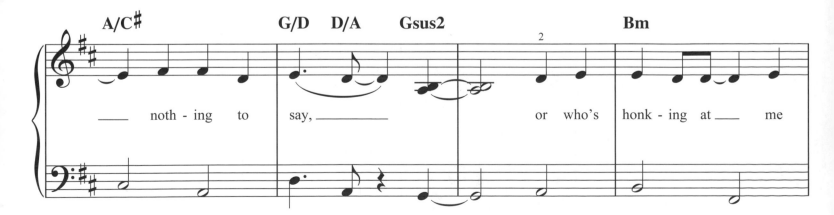

___ noth - ing to say, ___ or who's honk - ing at ___ me

from his Chev - ro - let! _____ One ___ day, I'm

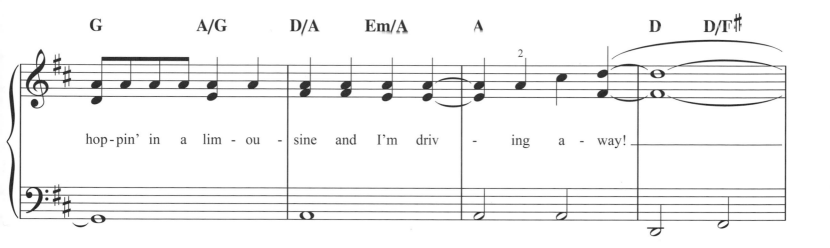

hop-pin' in a lim - ou - sine and I'm driv - ing a - way! _____

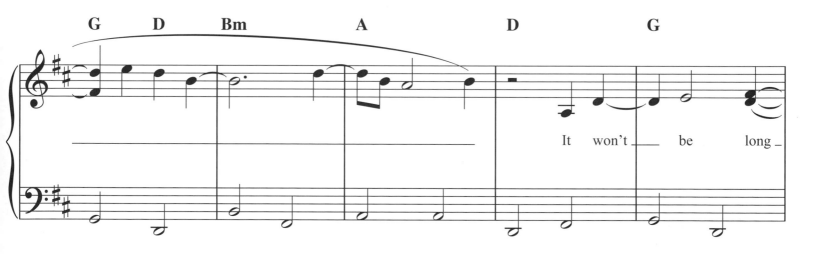

It won't ___ be long _

now. ___

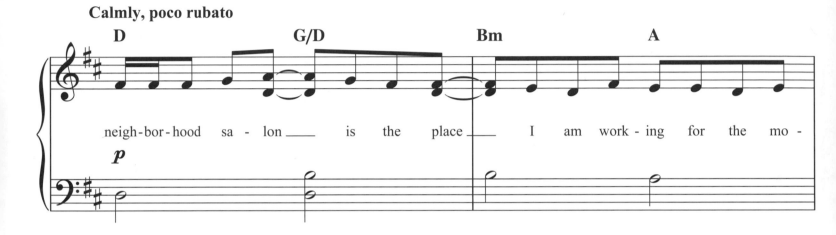

Calmly, poco rubato

neigh-bor-hood sa-lon ___ is the place ___ I am work-ing for the mo-

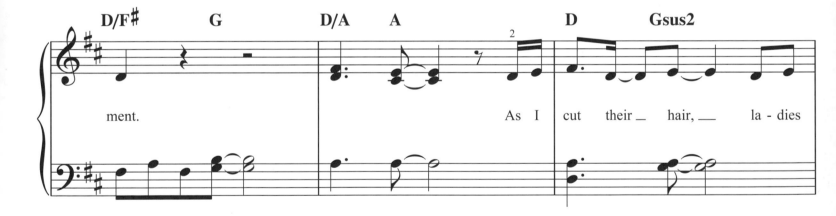

ment.   As I cut their ___ hair, ___ la-dies

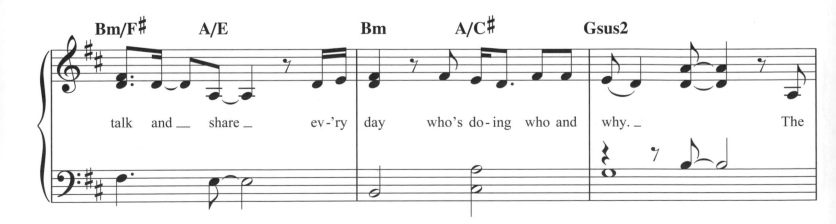

talk and ___ share ___ ev-'ry day who's do-ing who and why. ___ The

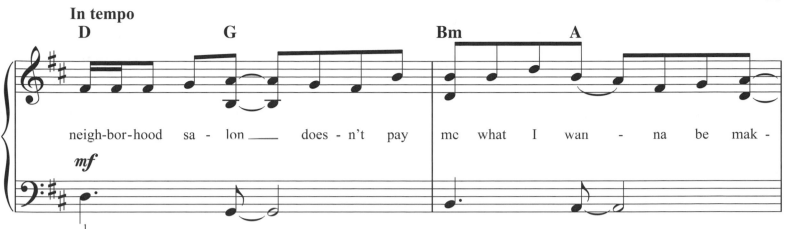

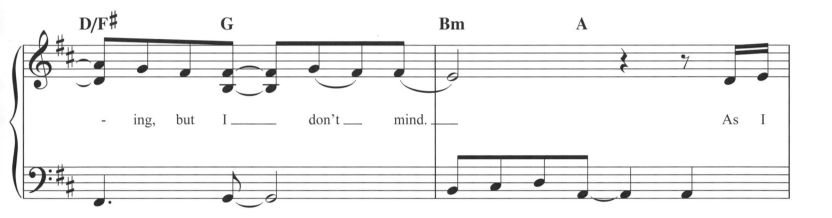

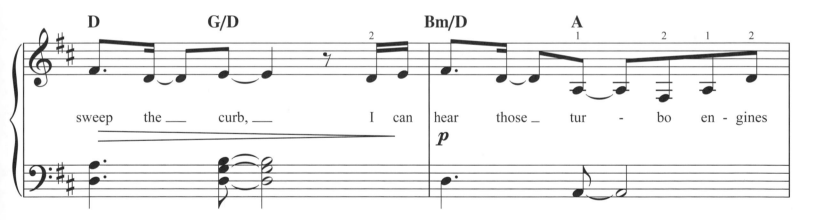

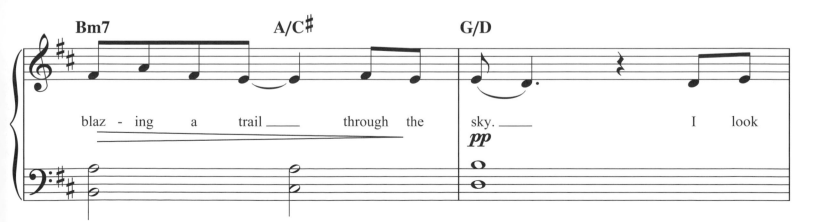

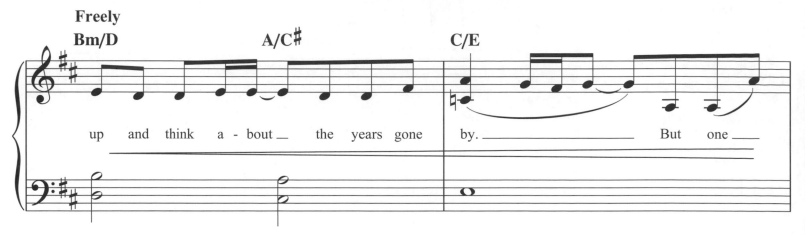

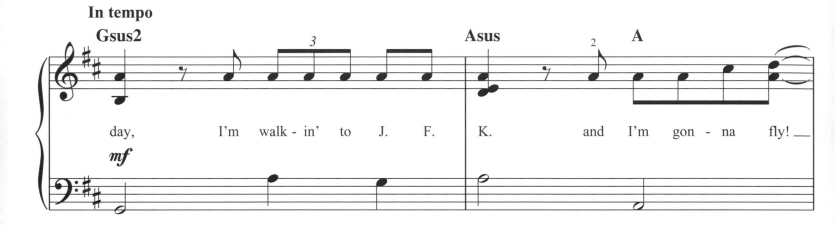

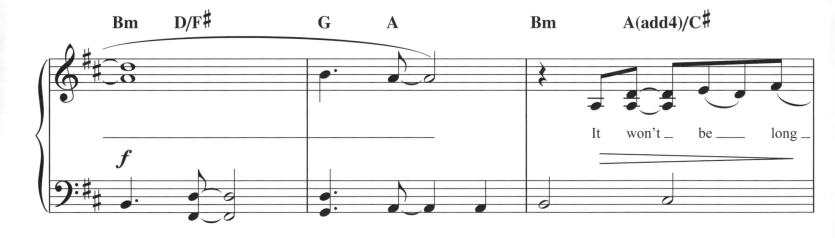

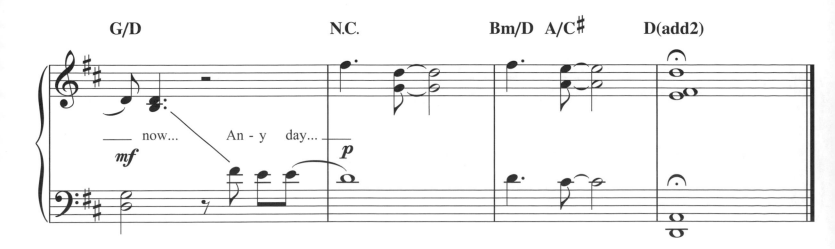

INÚTIL

Music and Lyrics by
LIN-MANUEL MIRANDA

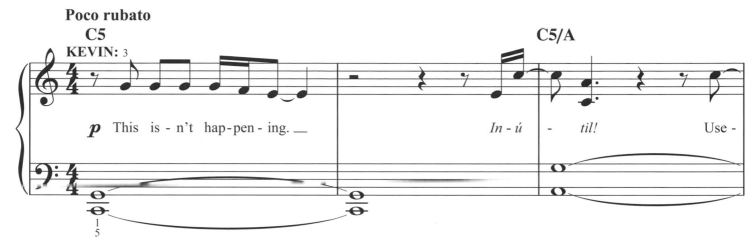

This isn't hap-pen-ing. _ In-ú-til! Use-

-less. Just like my fa-ther was _ be-fore _ me: In-ú-

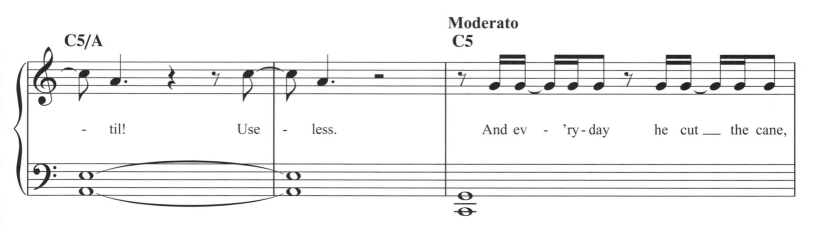

-til! Use-less. And ev-'ry-day he cut _ the cane,

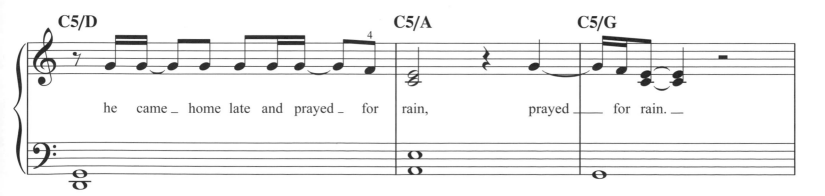

he came _ home late and prayed _ for rain, prayed _ for rain. _

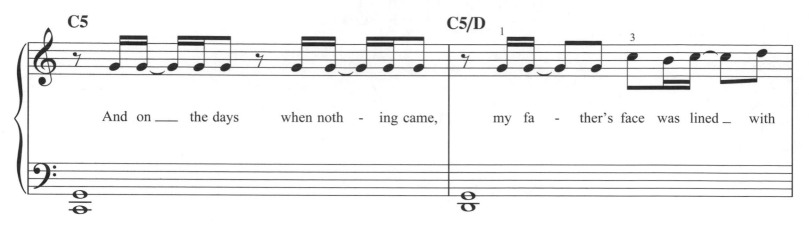

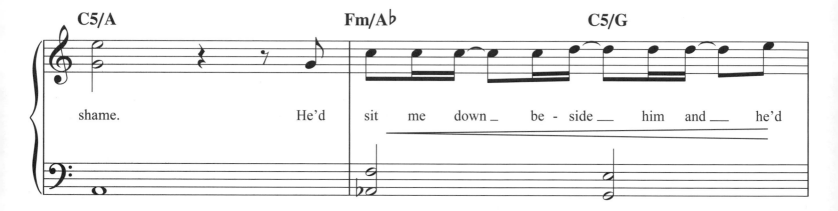

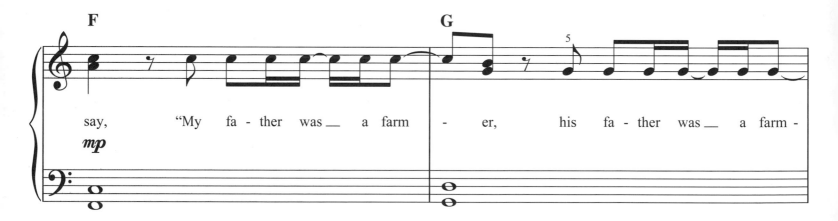

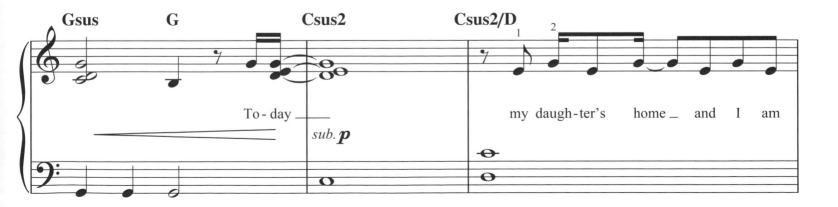

Am7 **Am7/E** **Gsus** **G** **Csus2**

use - less.   And as a ba - by she a - mazed

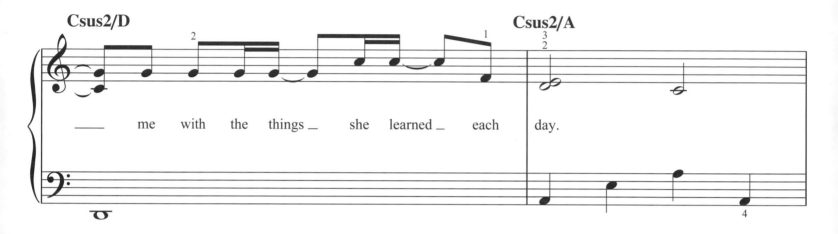

Csus2/D **Csus2/A**

me with the things she learned each day.

Gsus **G** **C**

She used to stay on the fire es -

Csus2/D **Csus2/A**

cape while all the oth - er kids would play.   And

I would stand be-side — her and I'd say: "I'm proud to be — your

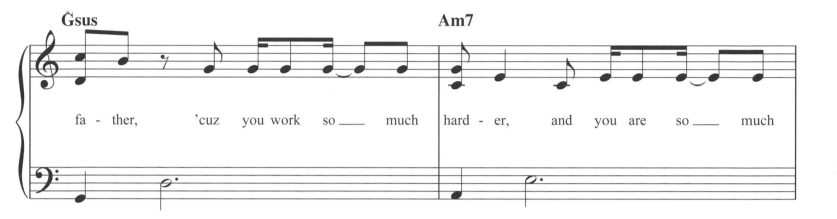

fa - ther, 'cuz you work so — much hard - er, and you are so — much

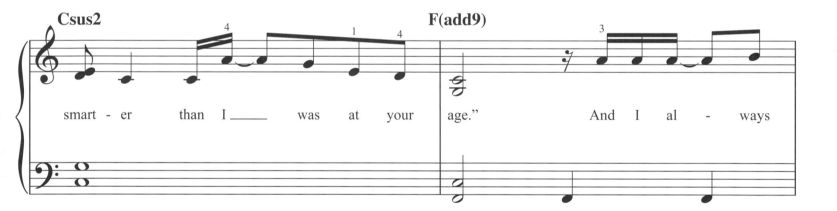

smart - er than I — was at your age." And I al - ways

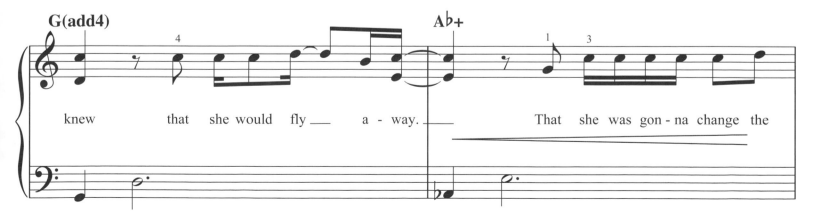

knew that she would fly — a - way. — That she was gon - na change the

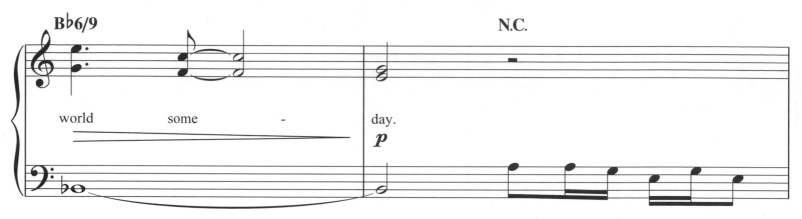

Bb6/9   **N.C.**

world   some - day.   *p*

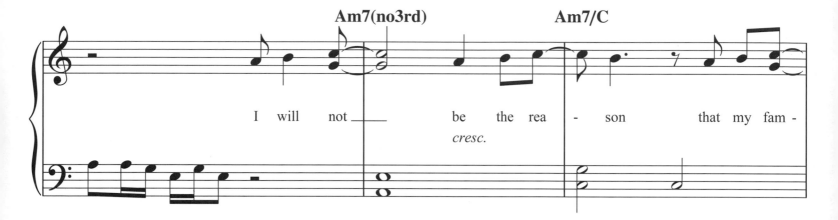

Am7(no3rd)   **Am7/C**

I will not   be the rea - son that my fam -
cresc.

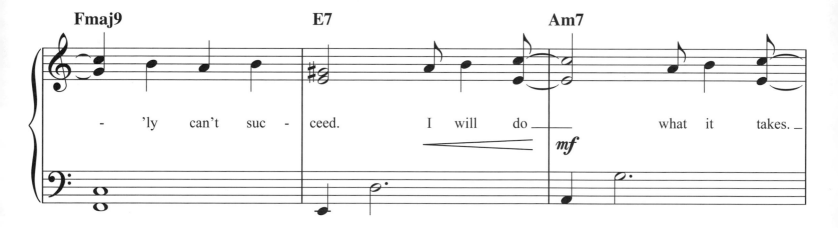

Fmaj9   **E7**   **Am7**

- 'ly can't suc - ceed. I will do   what it takes.   *mf*

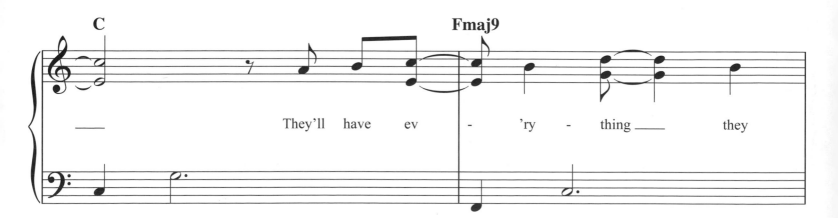

C   **Fmaj9**

They'll have ev - 'ry - thing   they

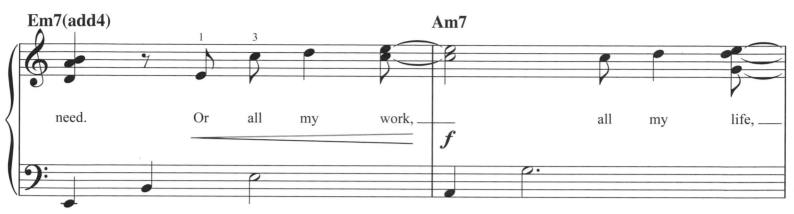

need. Or all my work, all my life, ___

___ ev - 'ry - thing ___ I've sac - ri - ficed

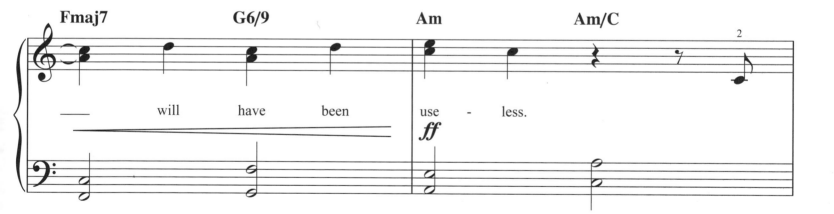

___ will have been use - less.

NO ME DIGA

Music and Lyrics by
LIN-MANUEL MIRANDA

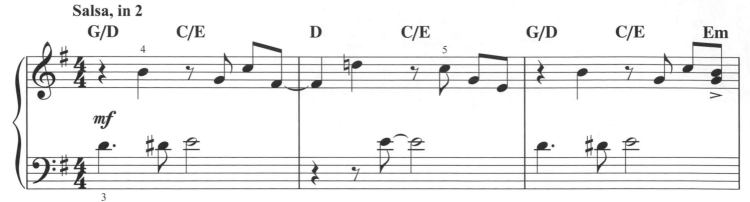

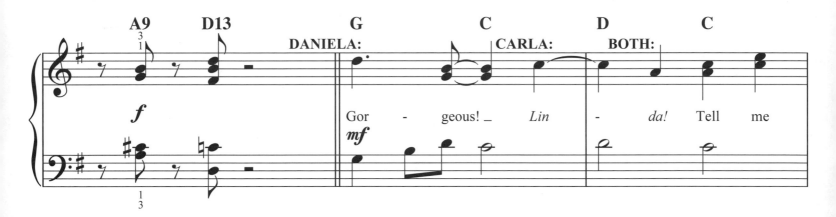

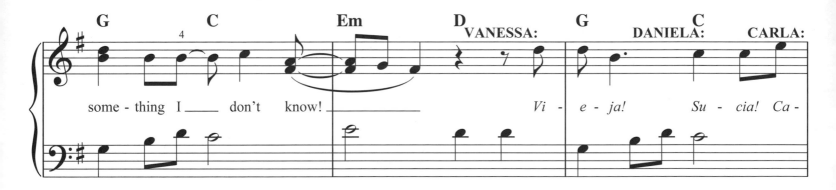

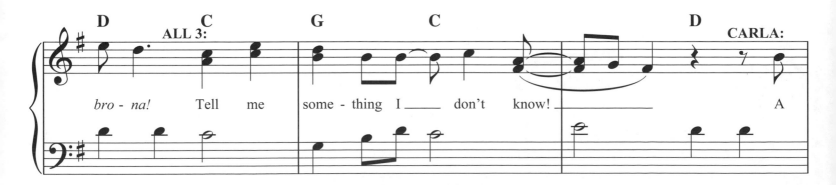

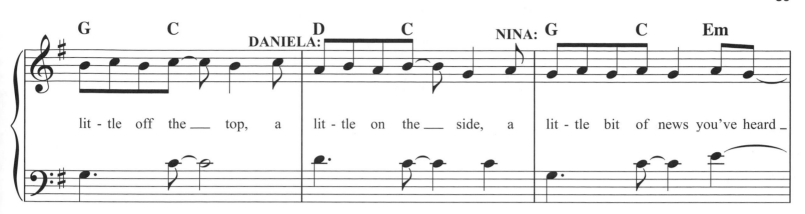

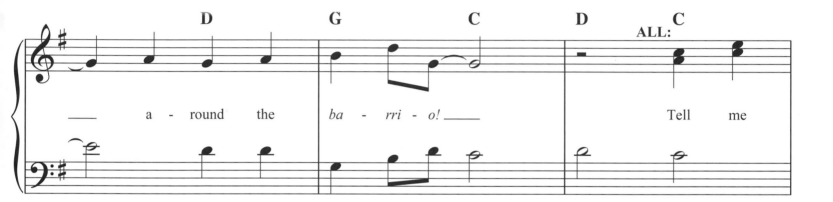

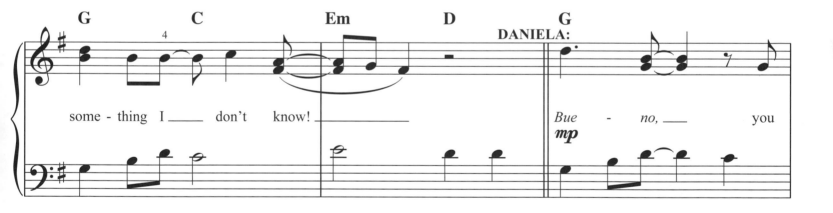

told me, Us - na - vi had sex __ with Yo - lan - da!

CARLA & NINA: **VANESSA:**

No me di - ga! Ay, *no!* He'd nev - er go out with a

skank like that! __ Please tell me you're jok - ing! O - kay! **DANIELA:** Just

want - ed to see __ what you'd say! **CARLA, DANIELA & NINA:** Tell me

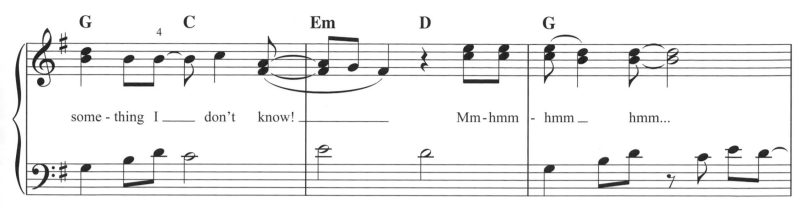

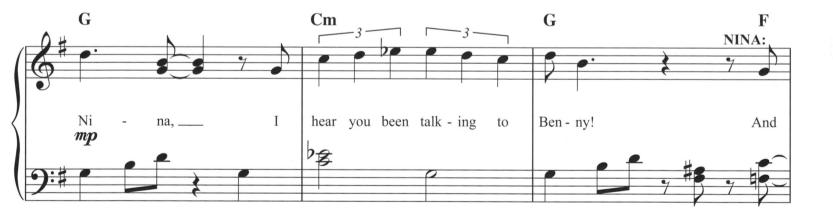

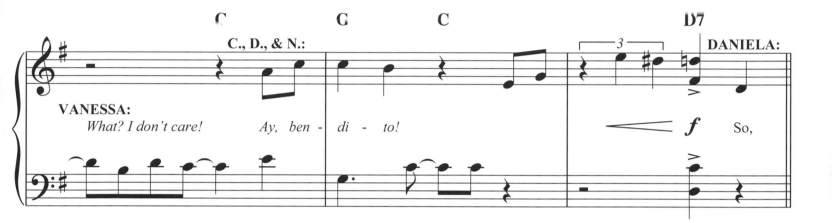

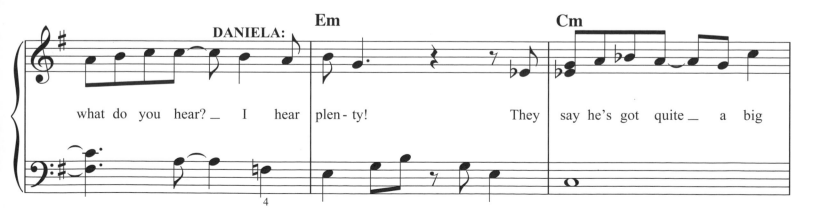

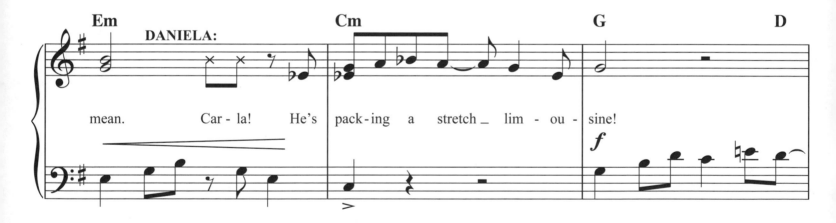

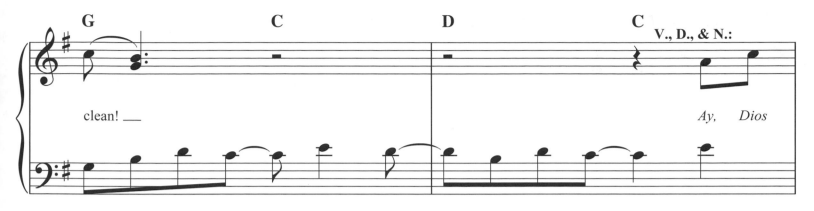

clean! —

V., D., & N.:

Ay, Dios

mi - o!

Bachata, l'istesso tempo

DANIELA:

Ni - na, se - ri - ous - ly, — we knew you'd be the one to

sub. **p**

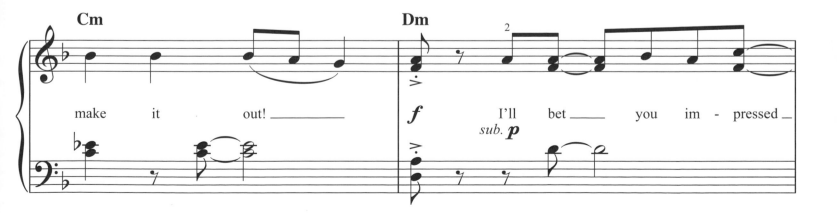

make it out! — I'll bet — you im - pressed —

f

sub. **p**

them __ all __ out __ west; __ you were al - ways the best, __

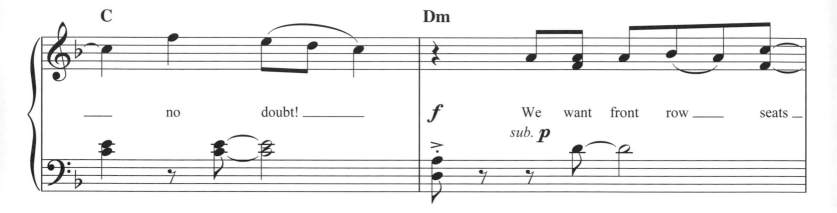

__ no doubt! _____ We want front row __ seats __

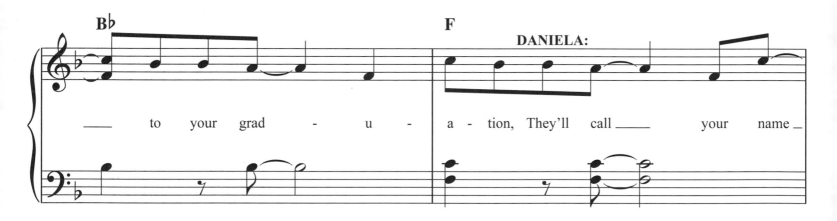

__ to your grad - u - a - tion, They'll call ____ your name __

DANIELA:

__ and we'll scream __ and shout! _____

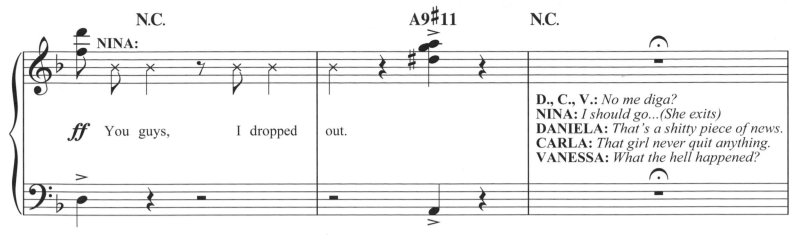

D., C., V.: *No me diga?*
NINA: *I should go...(She exits)*
DANIELA: *That's a shitty piece of news.*
CARLA: *That girl never quit anything.*
VANESSA: *What the hell happened?*

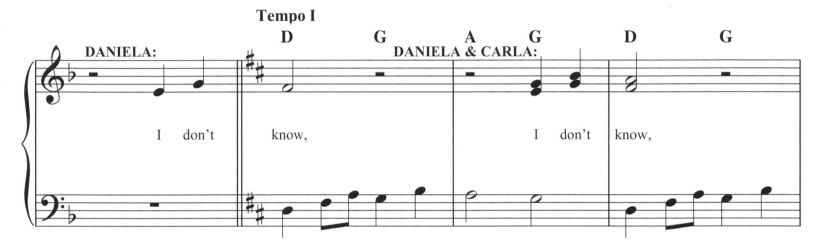

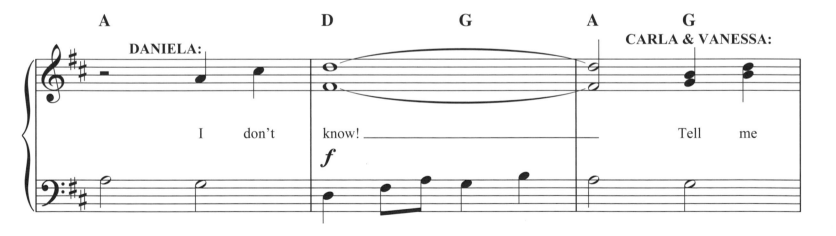

PACIENCIA Y FE

Music and Lyrics by
LIN-MANUEL MIRANDA

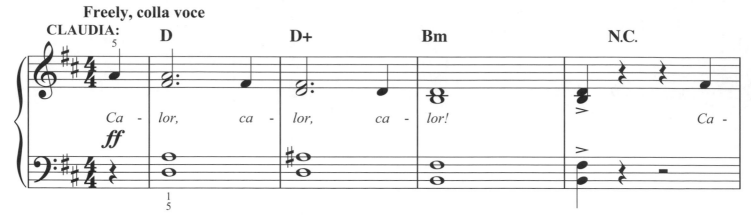

Freely, colla voce

CLAUDIA:

Ca - lor, ca - lor, ca - lor! Ca -

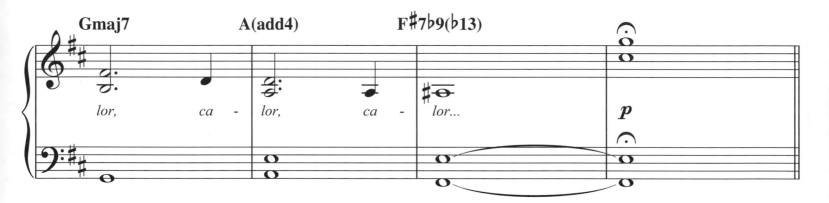

lor, ca - lor, ca - lor...

Salsa, in 2

Ay, __ Ma-má! The sum-mer's hot - test day!

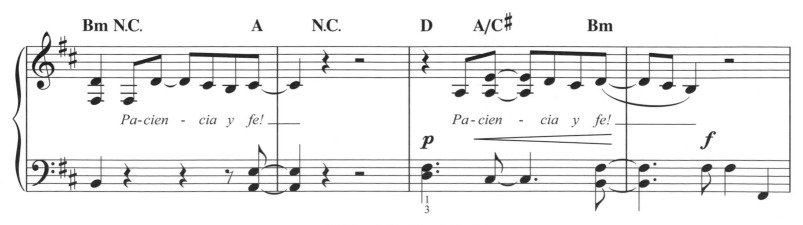

Pa-cien - cia y fe! Pa-cien - cia y fe!

Ay, ca-ra-jo, it's hot! But that's _ o-kay!

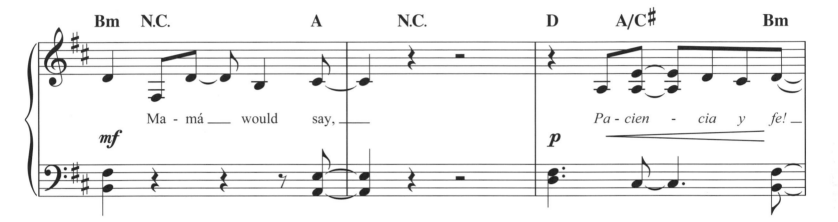

Ma-má _ would say, _ Pa-cien - cia y fe! _

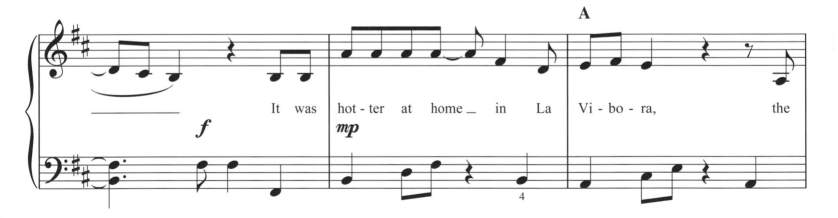

_____ It was hot-ter at home _ in La Vi-bo-ra, the

Wash-ing-ton Heights of Ha-va-na! _ A crowd-ed cit-y of fac-

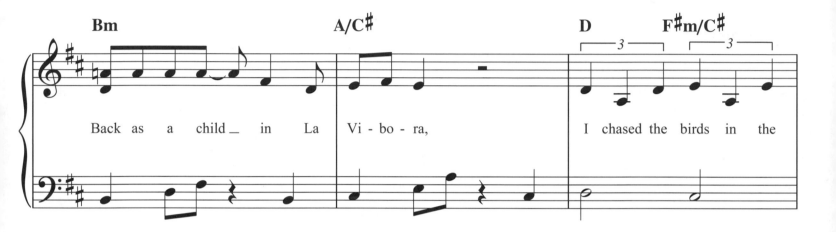

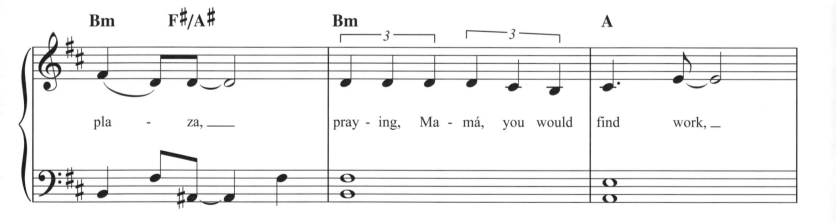

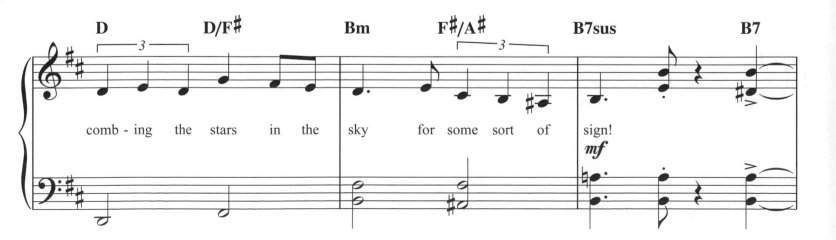

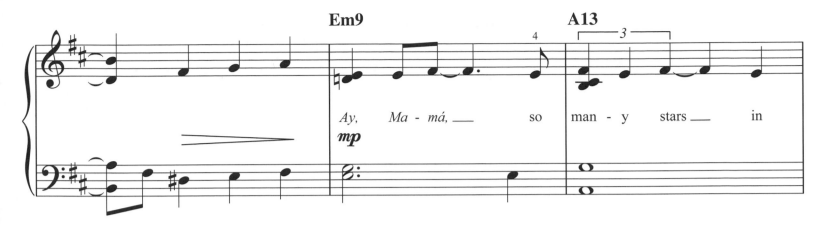

Em9   A13

Ay, Ma - má, ___ so man - y stars ___ in

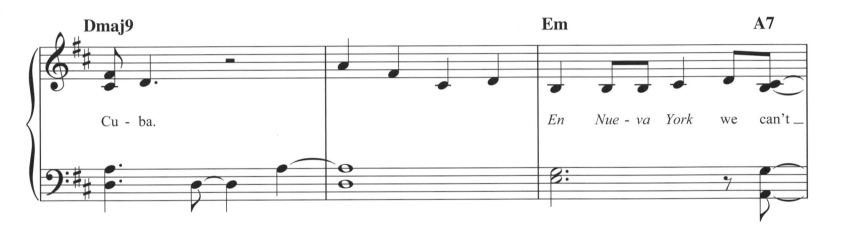

Dmaj9   Em   A7

Cu - ba.   *En Nue - va York we can't __*

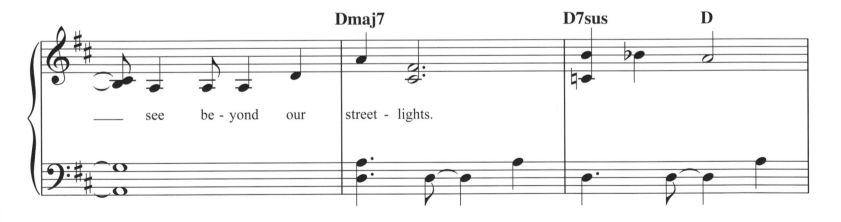

Dmaj7   D7sus   D

__ see be - yond our street - lights.

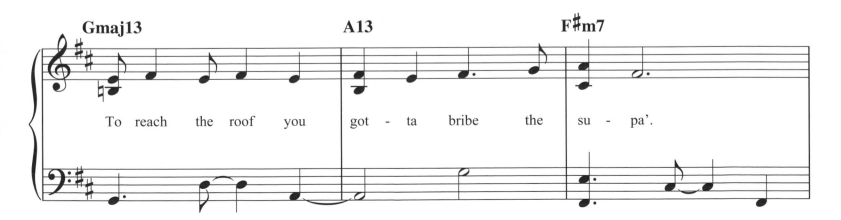

Gmaj13   A13   F#m7

To reach the roof you got - ta bribe the su - pa'.

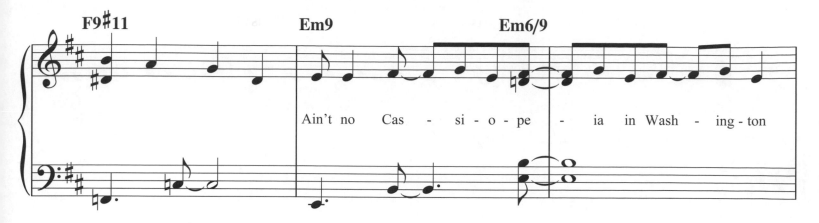

Ain't no Cas - si - o - pe - ia in Wash - ing - ton

Heights, but ain't no food — in La — Vi - bo - ra!

I re - mem - ber nights, an - ger in the streets, hun - ger at the

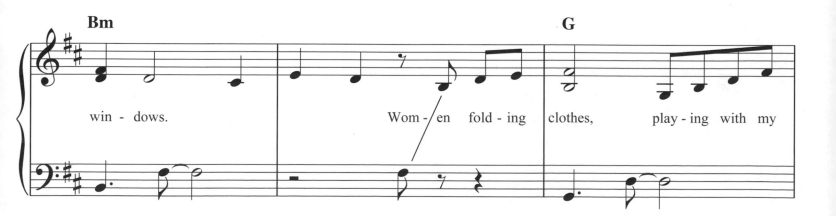

win - dows. Wom - en fold - ing clothes, play - ing with my

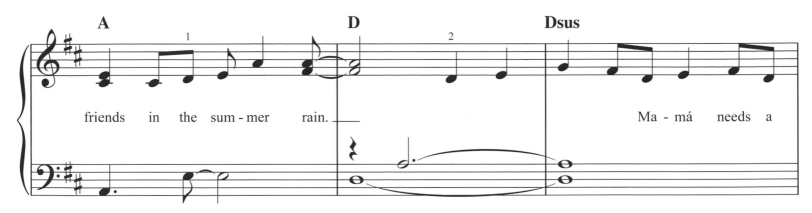

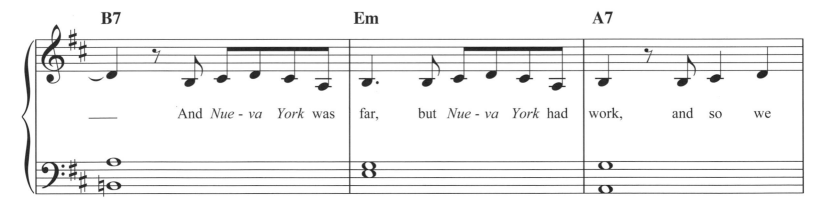

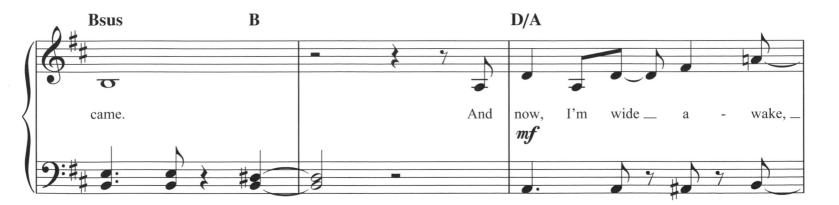

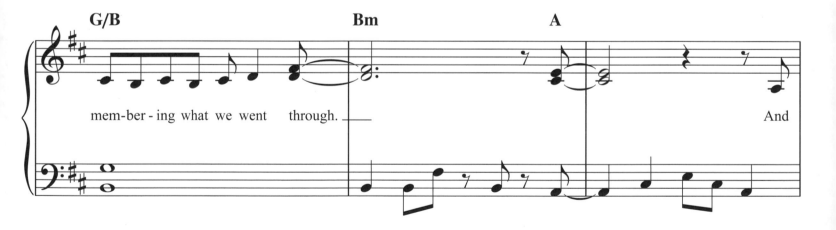

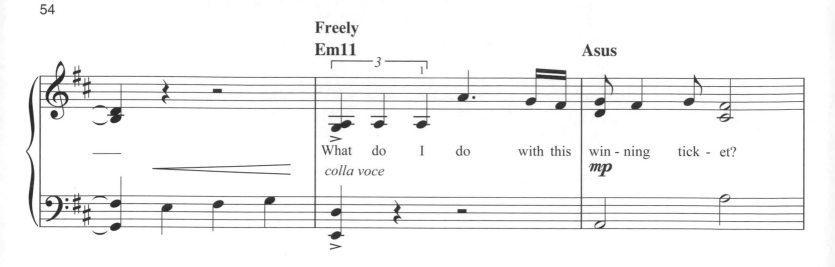

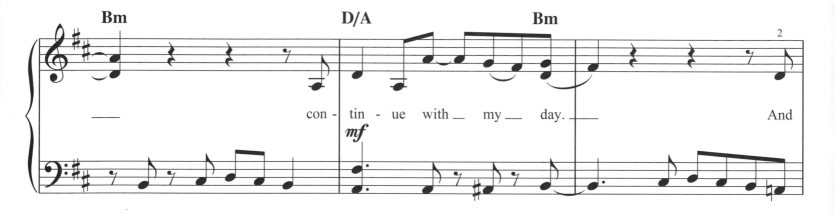

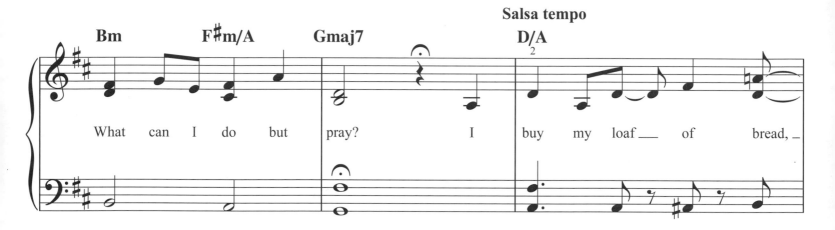

55

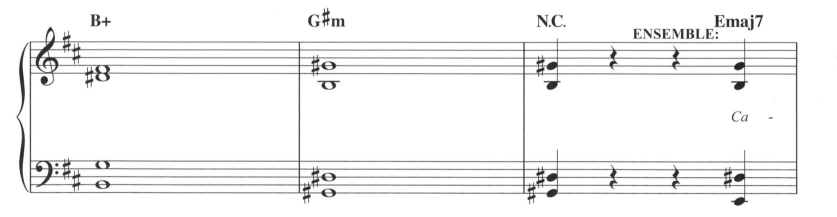

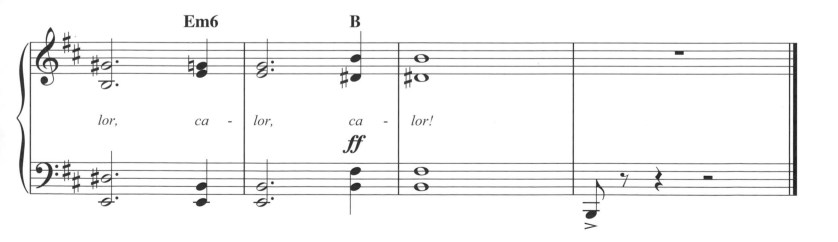

WHEN YOU'RE HOME

Music and Lyrics by
LIN-MANUEL MIRANDA

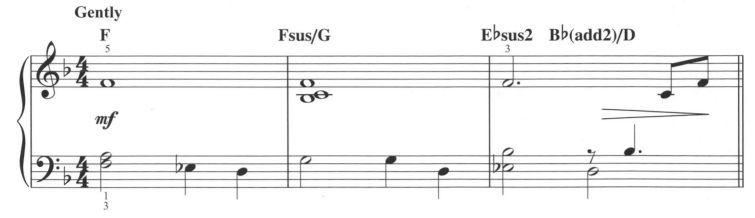

I used to think _ we lived at the top _ of the world, _ when the world was just a

sub-way map. _ And the One-slash-Nine _ climbed a dot-ted line _ to my

place. There's no nine _ train now. _ Right. I used to think _ the

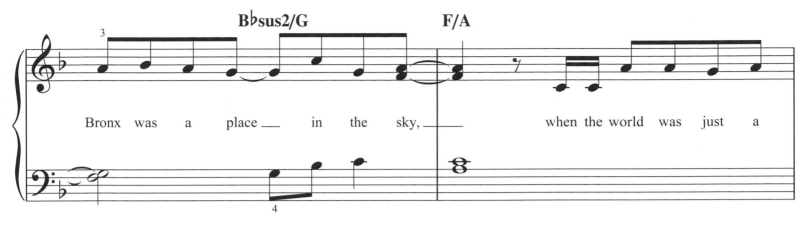

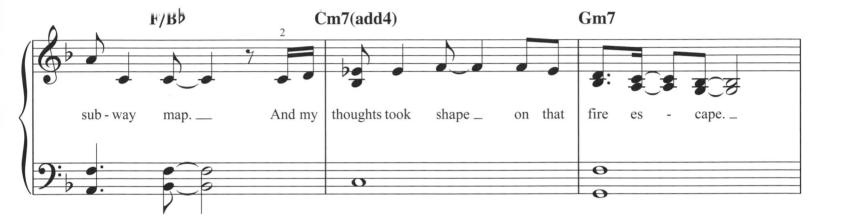

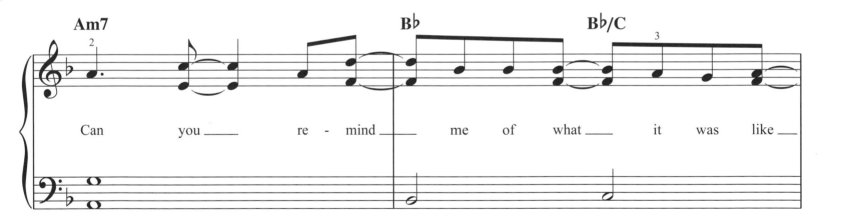

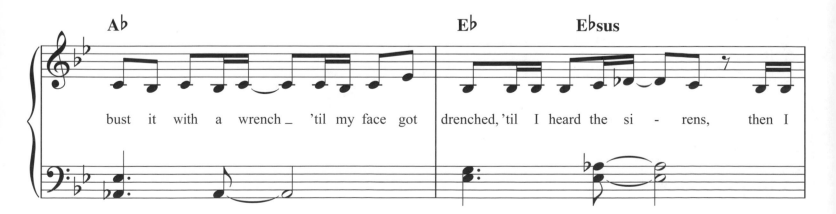

ran like ___ hell! ___ Yeah, I ran ___ like hell! ___ To your

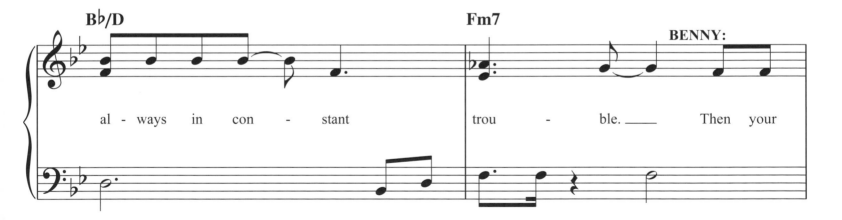

fa-ther's dis-patch win-dow, "Hey, let me in, yo! They're com-ing to get me!" You were

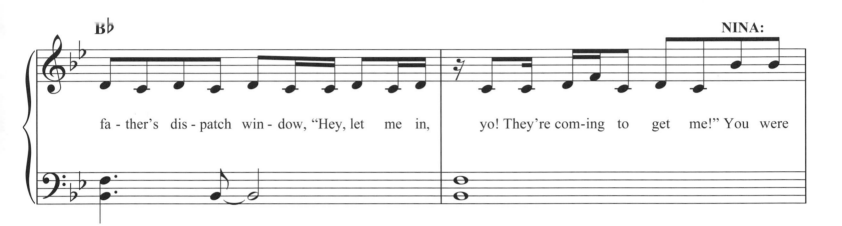

al - ways in con - stant trou - ble. ___ Then your

dad would act all snide, but he let me hide. ___ You'd be there in - side. ___ Life was

eas - ier ___ then. ___ Ni - na, ev - 'ry - thing ___ is eas - i - er when you're

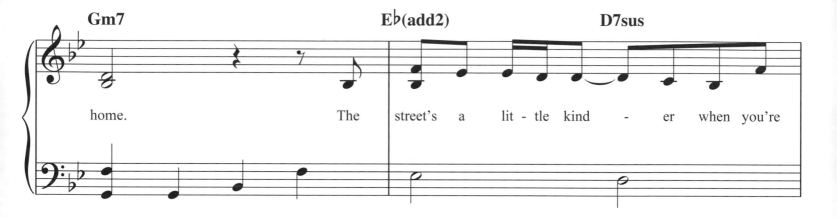

home. The street's a lit - tle kind ___ er when you're

home. Can't you ___ see ___ that the day ___

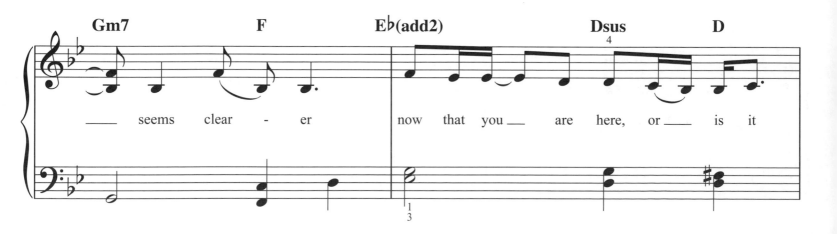

___ seems clear - er now that you ___ are here, or ___ is it

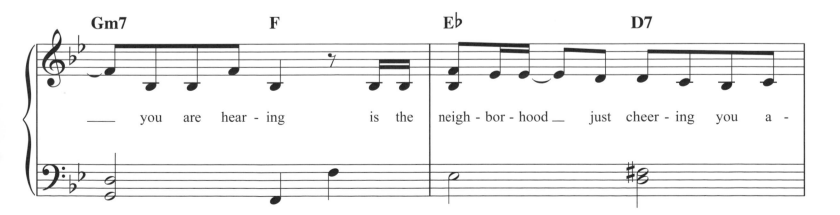

Cm9   NINA: BENNY: **G♭m7♭5**   NINA: **B7**

long. Don't say _____ that. What's wrong? _ Don't say that!

Salsa, double time

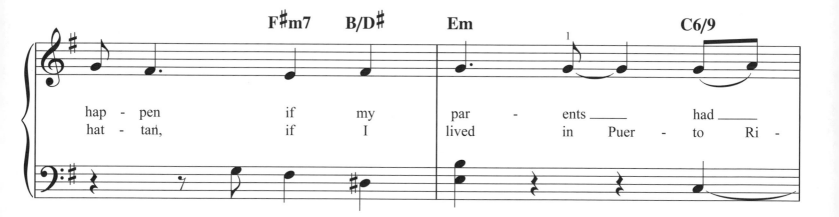

Em   **D6**   **Cmaj7**   **B+**

When I _____ was young - er, I'd i - mag - ine what would

Who would _ I be if I had nev - er seen Man -

F♯m7   **B/D♯**   **Em**   1   **C6/9**

hap - pen if my par - ents _____ had _____

hat - tan, if I lived in Puer - to Ri -

1.

G6/9   2

stayed in Puer - to Ri - co.

- co with my peo -

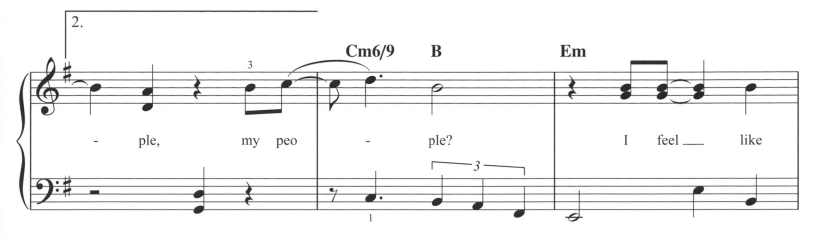

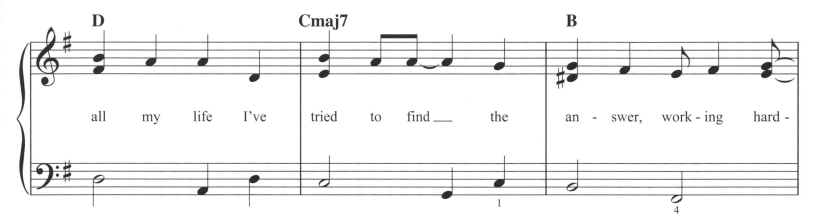

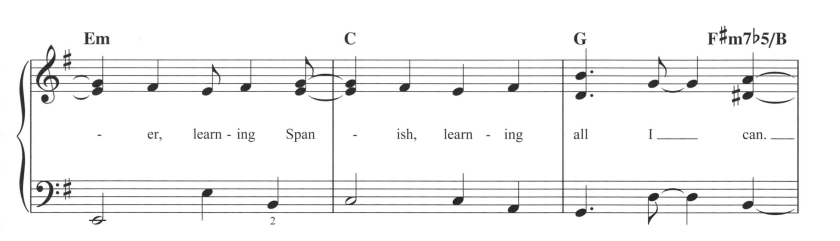

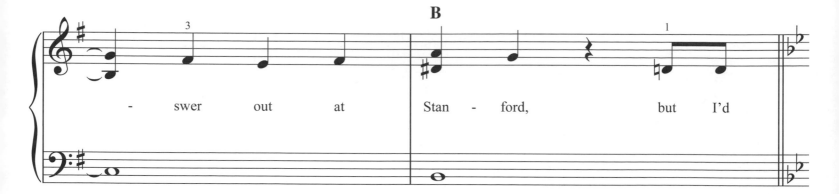

- swer out at Stan - ford, but I'd

Half-time, slowing down

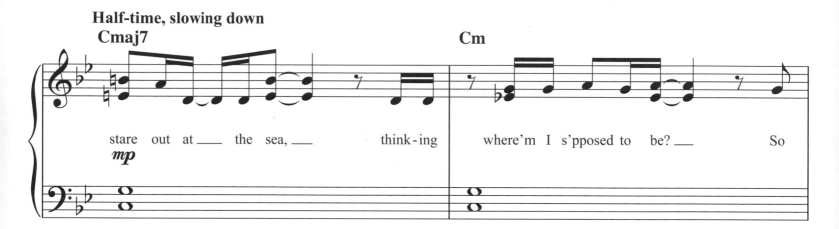

stare out at ___ the sea, ___ think-ing where'm I s'pposed to be? ___ So

mp

please don't say you're proud of me when I've lost my ___ way. _____

A tempo

Then can I say, I

BENNY:

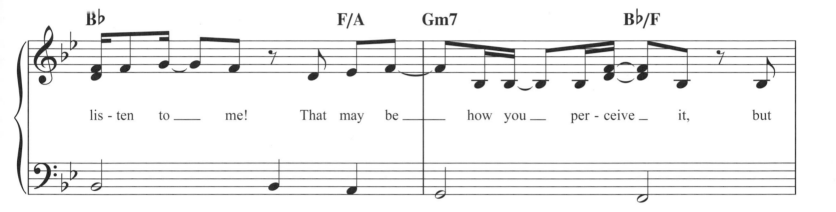

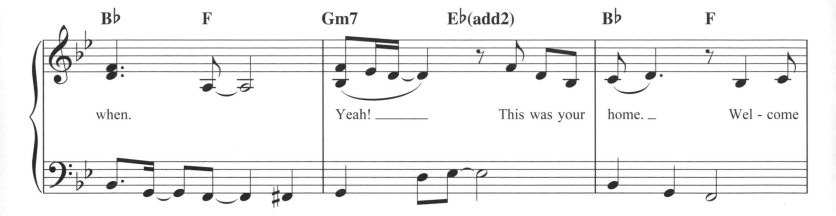

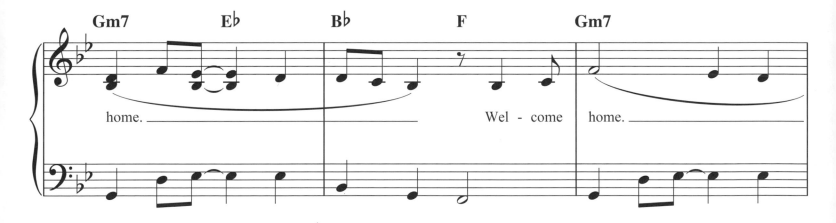

WHEN THE SUN GOES DOWN

Music and Lyrics by
LIN-MANUEL MIRANDA

Pop Ballad

When the sun goes _____ down, you're gon-na need a

flash-light. You're gon-na need a can-dle. I think I can man-age

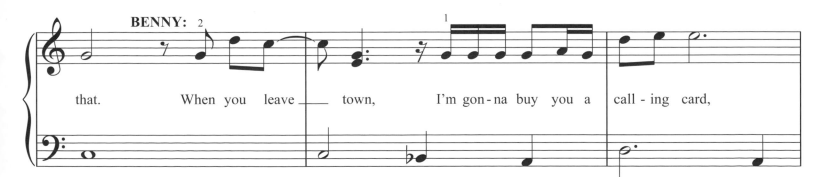

that. When you leave _____ town, I'm gon-na buy you a call-ing card,

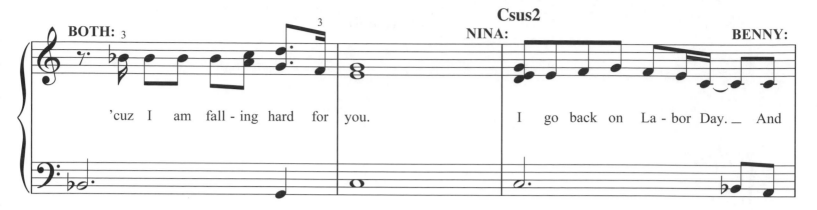

BOTH:

'cuz I am fall-ing hard for you.

Csus2

NINA:

I go back on La-bor Day. __ And

BENNY:

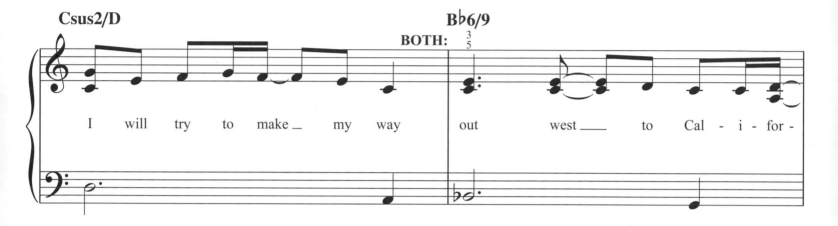

Csus2/D

I will try to make __ my way

Bb6/9

BOTH:

out west __ to Cal - i - for -

C

- nia.

BENNY:

So we've got this

Csus2

sum - mer,

NINA:

and we've got each

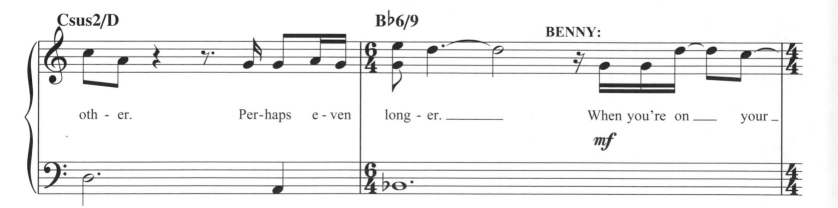

Csus2/D

oth - er. Per-haps e - ven

Bb6/9

long - er. _____

BENNY:

When you're on __ your __

mf

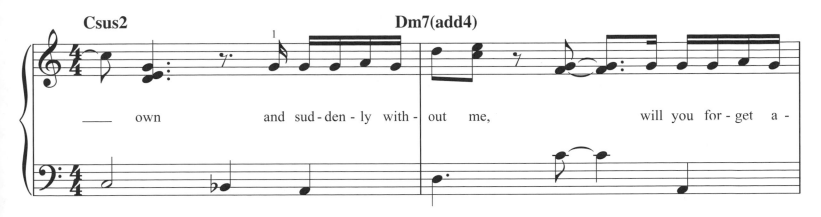

own and sud-den-ly with-out me, will you for-get a-

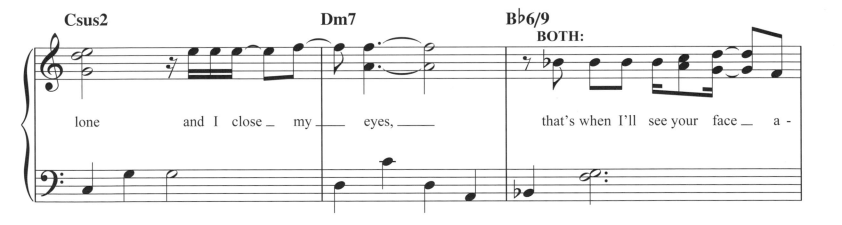

bout me? I could-n't if I tried. _____ When I'm all _____ a-

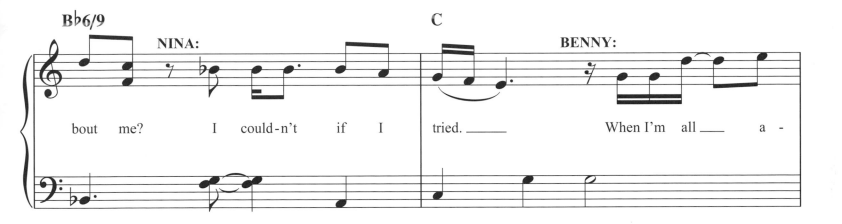

lone and I close _ my _ eyes, _____ that's when I'll see your face _ a-

gain. And when you're _____ gone, you

know that I'll ___ be wait - ing, when you're ___ gone. ___ But you're here ___

NINA:

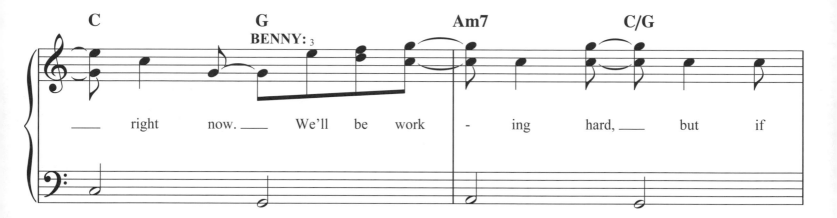

___ right now. ___ We'll be work - ing hard, ___ but if

BENNY:

we should drift ___ a - part, ___ let me take this ___ mo - ment just to

say, you are gon - na change the world ___ some day.

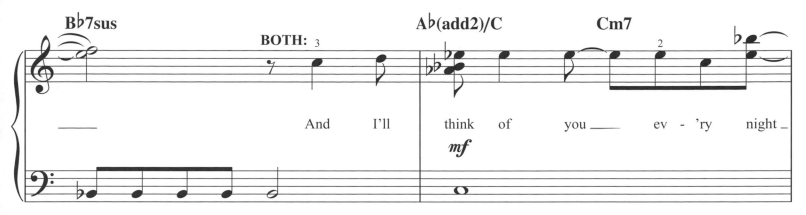

And I'll think of you ev - 'ry night

at the same time: when the sun goes

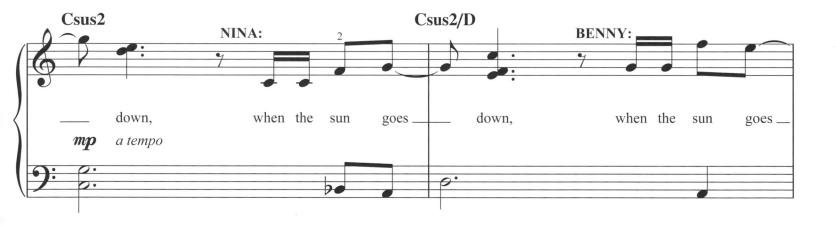

down, when the sun goes down, when the sun goes

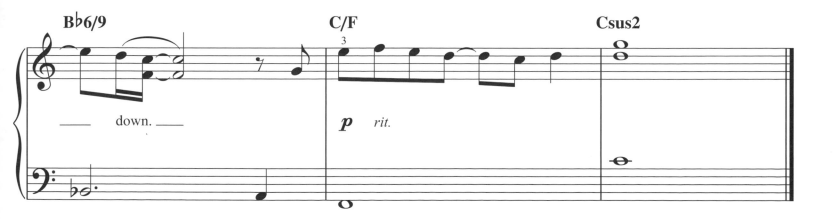

down.

SUNRISE

Music and Lyrics by
LIN-MANUEL MIRANDA

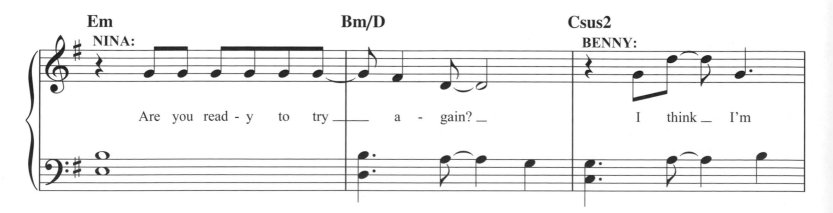

NINA: Are you read-y to try a - gain? **BENNY:** I think I'm

read - y.   NINA:*Okay...*   *Here we go...*   *Es - qui - na.*
                                                                  BENNY: Cor- ner.

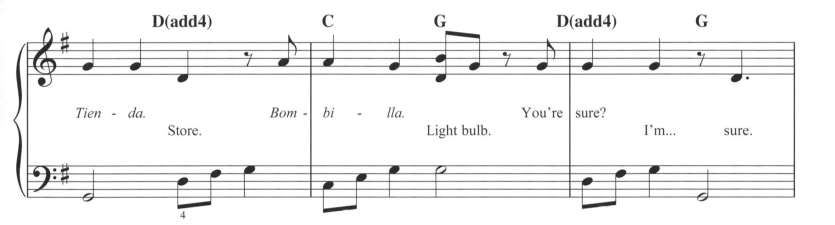

Tien - da.   *Bom - bi - lla.*   You're sure?   I'm...   sure.
Store.   Light bulb.

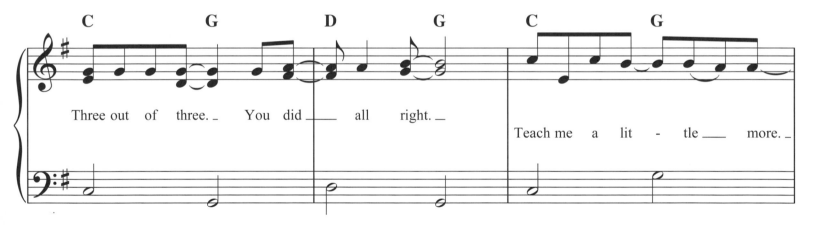

Three out of three. _   You did __ all right. _   Teach me a lit - tle __ more. _

Freely, colla voce

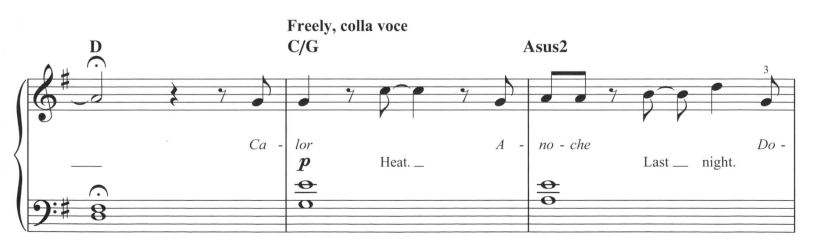

_____   *Ca - lor*   *A - no - che*   *Do -*
                          Heat. _   Last __ night.

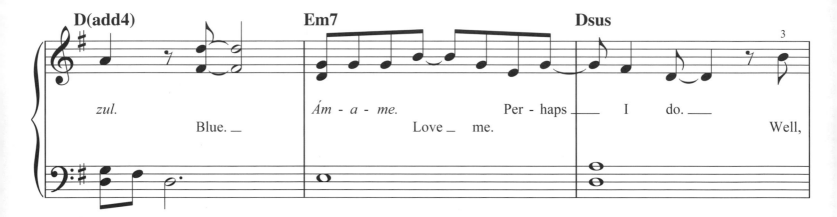

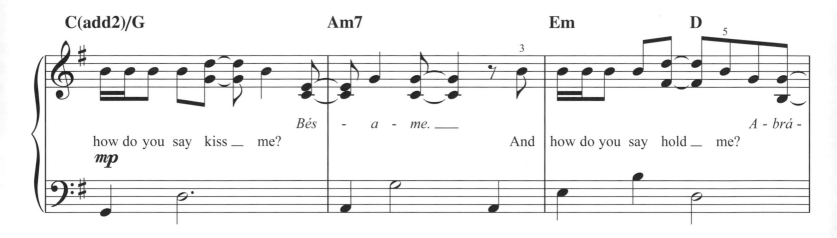

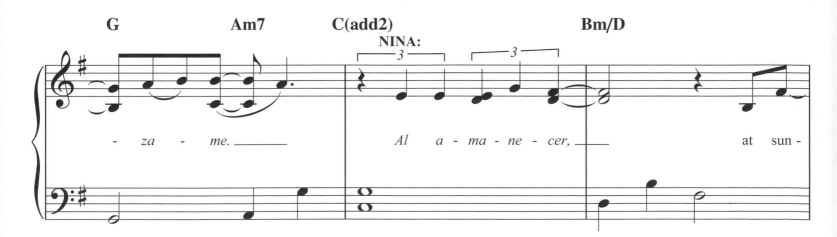

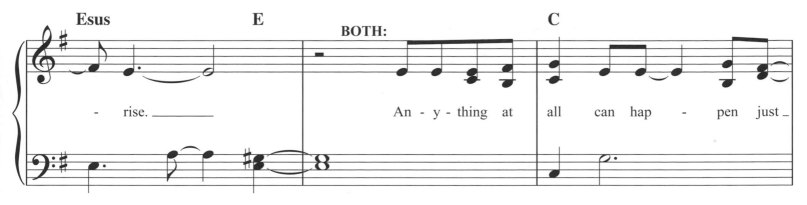

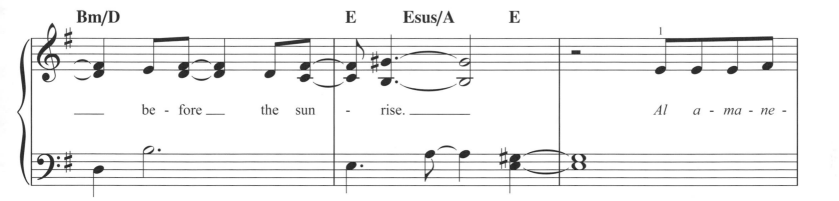

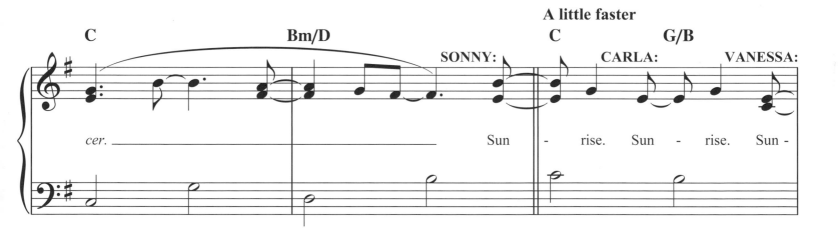

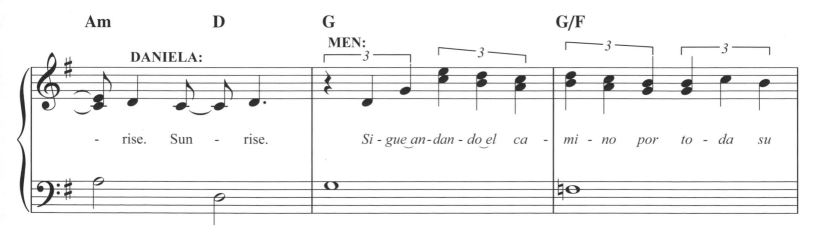

76

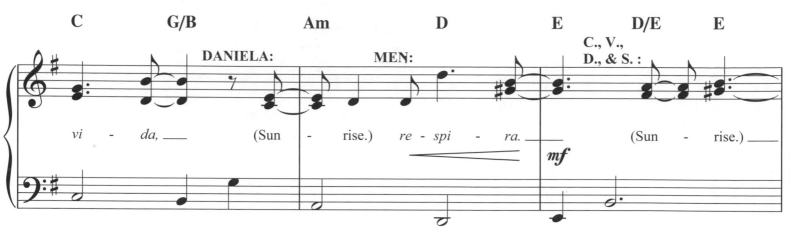

A little faster

you? So how do you say help ___ me? *A - yú -*

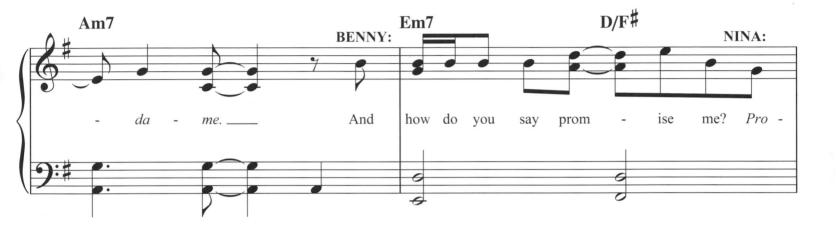

- da - me. ___ And how do you say prom - ise me? *Pro -*

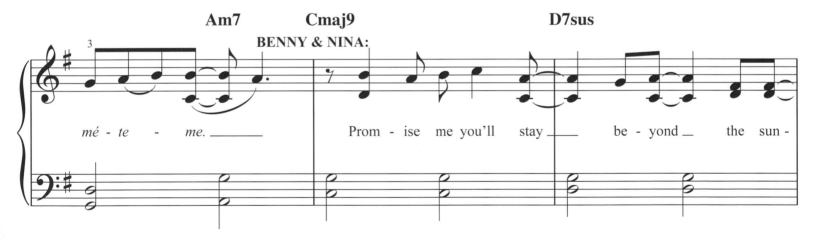

mé - te - me. ___ Prom - ise me you'll stay ___ be - yond ___ the sun -

- rise. ___ I don't care at all what peo - ple say ___

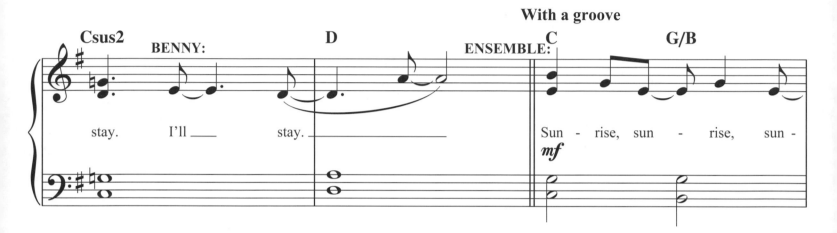

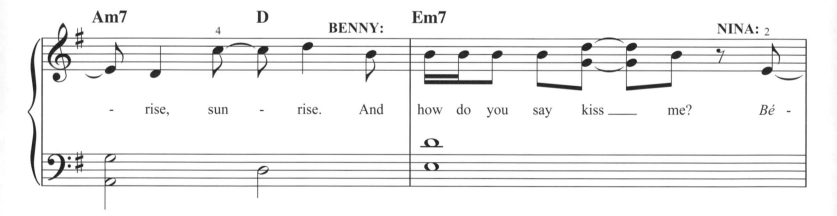

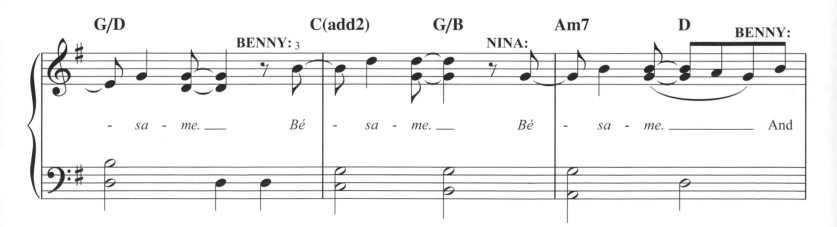

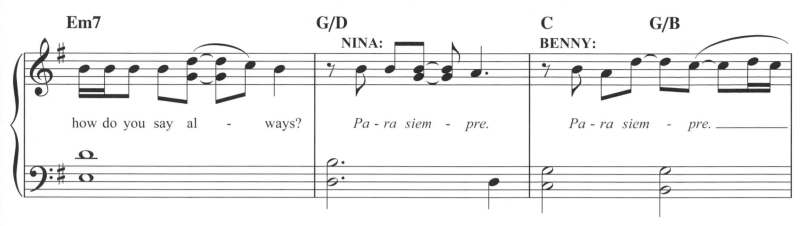

Em7   **G/D**   **C**   **G/B**

NINA: BENNY:

how do you say al - ways?   *Pa - ra siem - pre.*   *Pa - ra siem - pre.* ___

Am   **D**   **Em7**   **G/D**

NINA: BENNY:

___   *Al a - ma - ne - cer.* ___ *Al a - ma - ne - cer.*

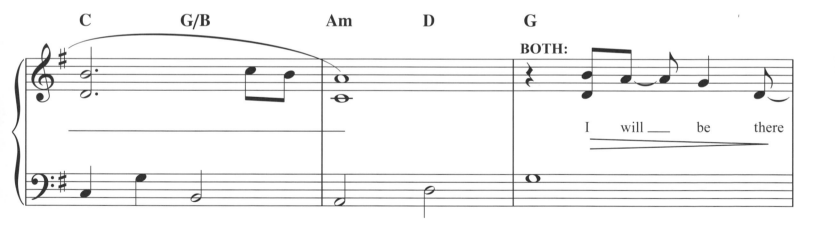

C   **G/B**   **Am**   **D**   **G**

BOTH:

___   I will ___ be there

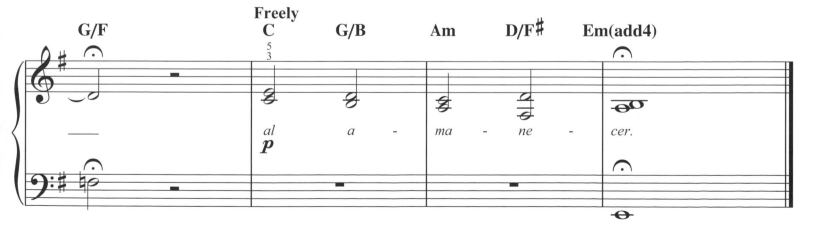

G/F   **Freely**   **C**   **G/B**   **Am**   **D/F#**   **Em(add4)**

___   *al*   *a -*   *ma -*   *ne -*   *cer.*

p

EVERYTHING I KNOW

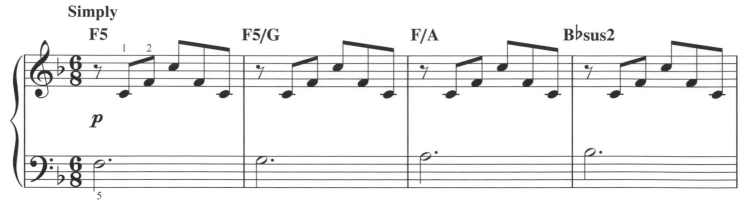

Music and Lyrics by
LIN-MANUEL MIRANDA

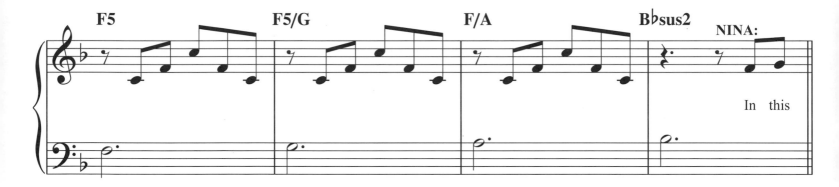

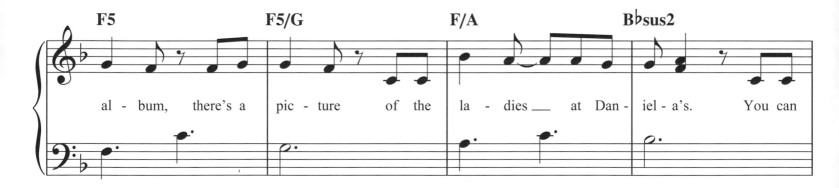

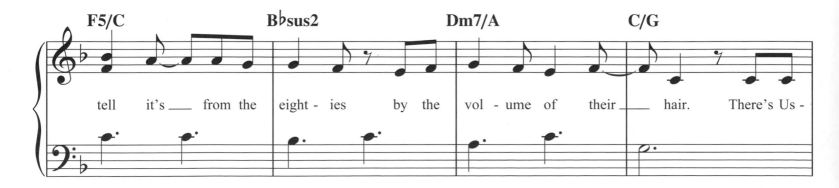

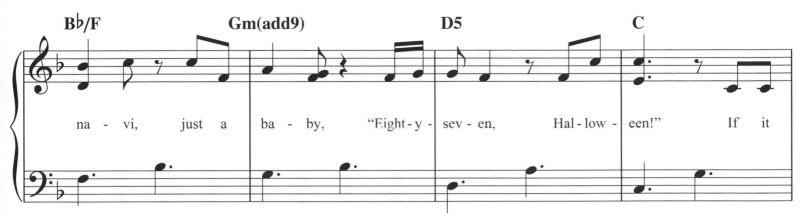

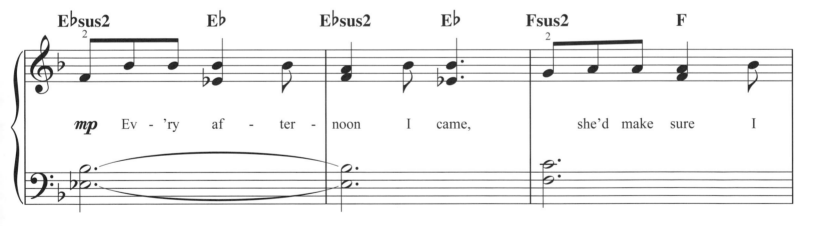

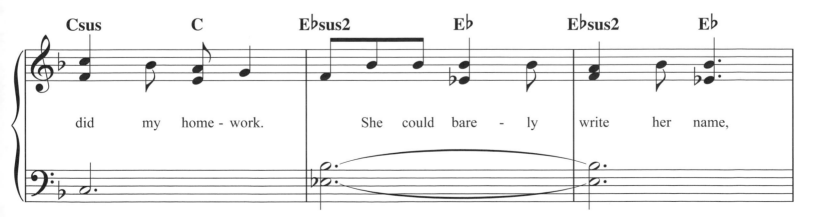

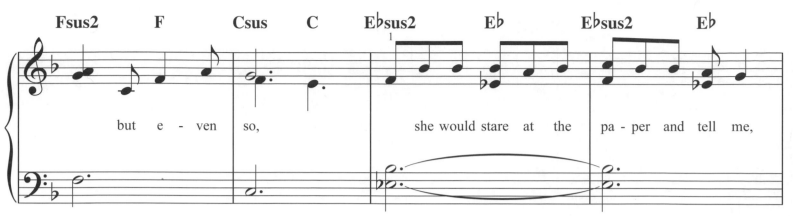

but e - ven so, she would stare at the pa - per and tell me,

"Bue - no, let's re - view, why don't you tell me ev - 'ry - thing you _

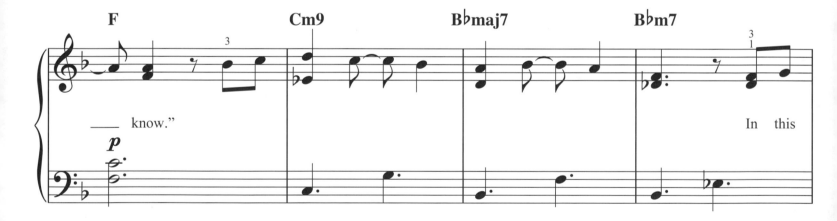

_ know." In this

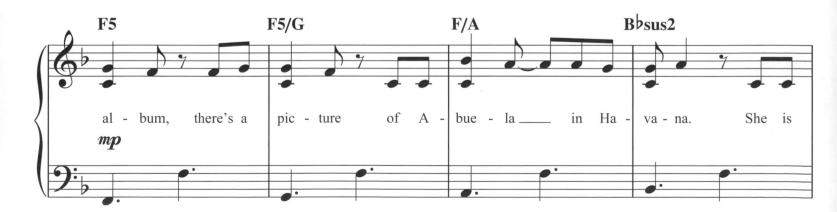

al - bum, there's a pic - ture of A - bue - la _ in Ha - va - na. She is

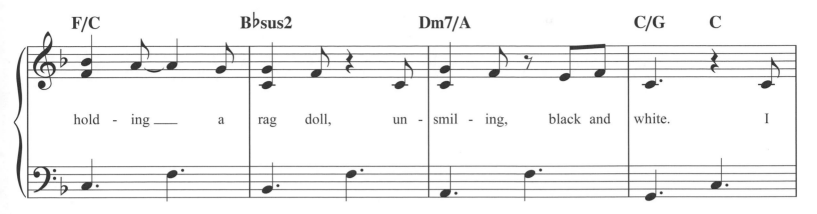

hold - ing ___ a rag doll, un - smil - ing, black and white. I

won - der what she's think - ing. Does she know that she'll be leav - ing for the

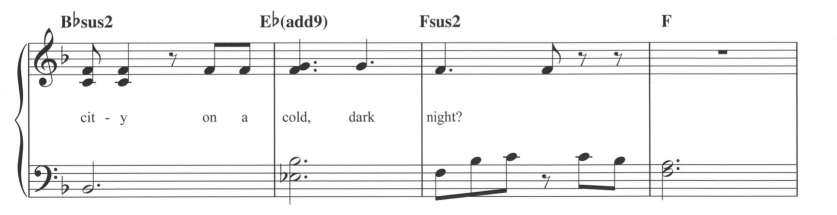

cit - y on a cold, dark night?

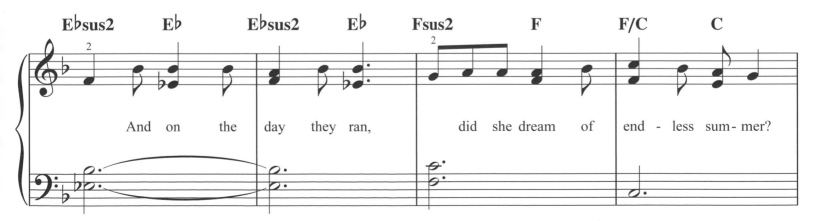

And on the day they ran, did she dream of end - less sum - mer?

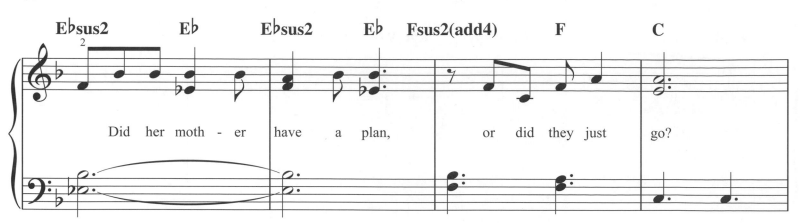

Did her moth - er have a plan, or did they just go?

Did some-bod - y sit her down _ and say, "Claud - ia, get read - y to

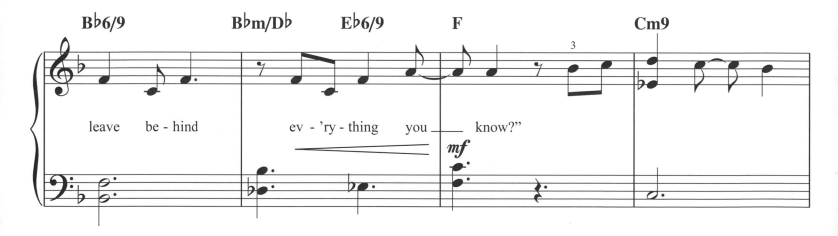

leave be - hind ev - 'ry - thing you _ know?"

Ev - 'ry - thing I _ know. _

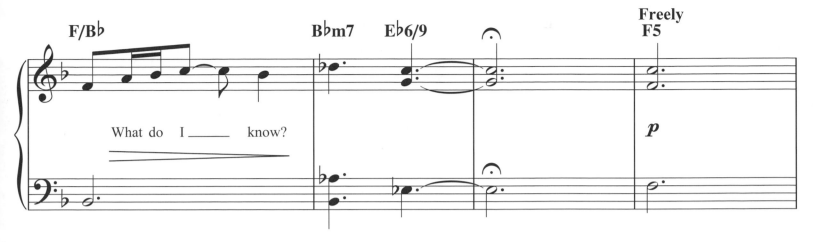

F/B♭   **B♭m7**   **E♭6/9**   **Freely / F5**

What do I ____ know?

p

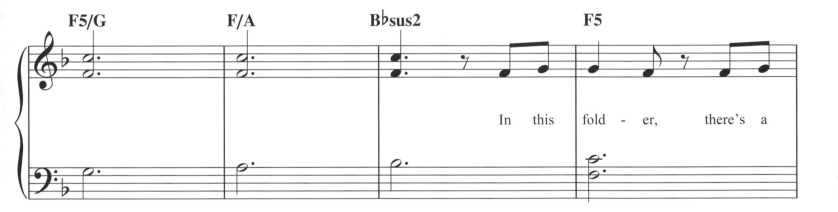

F5/G   **F/A**   **B♭sus2**   **F5**

In this fold - er, there's a

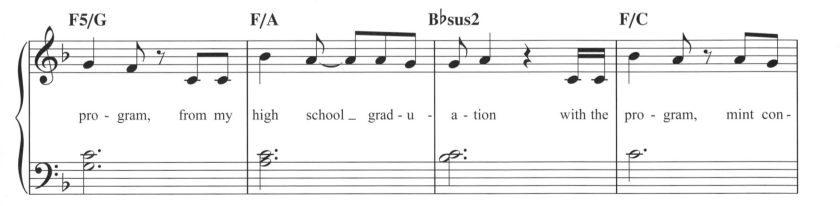

F5/G   **F/A**   **B♭sus2**   **F/C**

pro - gram, from my high school grad-u - a - tion with the pro - gram, mint con -

B♭sus2   **Dm/A**   **Csus**   **A tempo / F**

di - tion, and a star be - side my name. Here's a pic - ture of my

parents as I left for Cal - i - for - nia. She saved ev - 'ry - thing we

cresc. *mf*

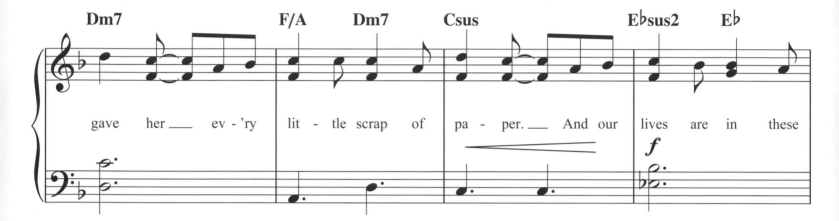

gave her ___ ev -'ry lit - tle scrap of pa - per. ___ And our lives are in these

f

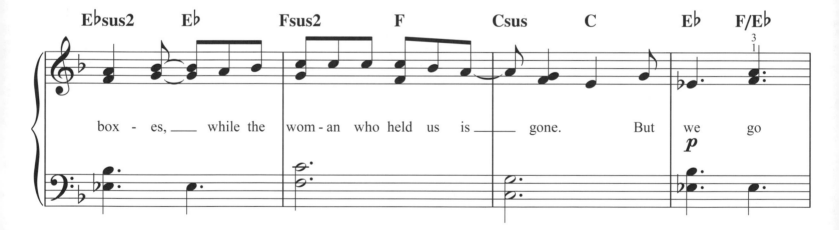

box - es, ___ while the wom - an who held us is ___ gone. But we go

p

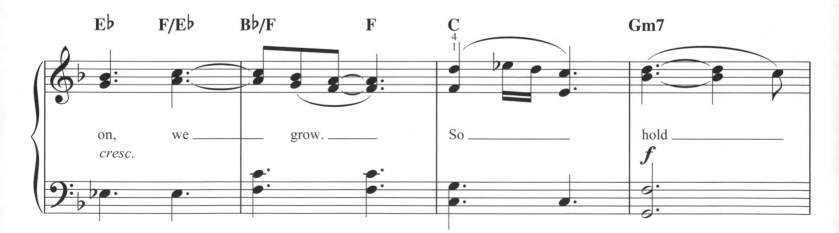

on, we ___ grow. ___ So ___ hold ___

cresc. *f*

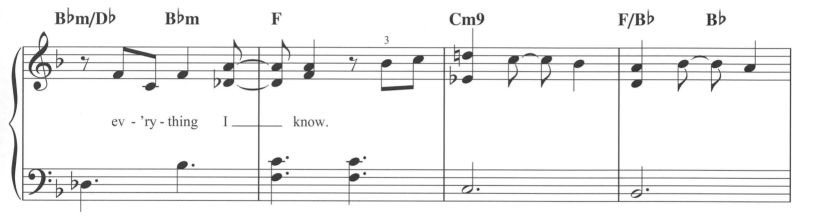

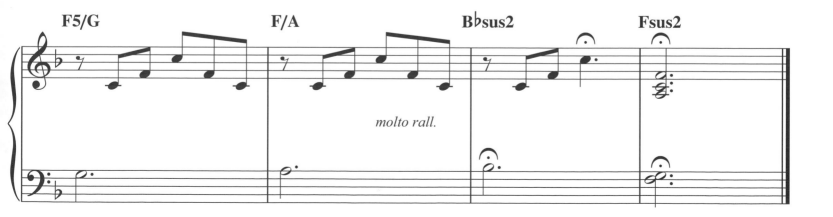